@ 7/15/2020

Creative Culture

HUMAN~CENTERED
INTERACTION, DESIGN, & INSPIRATION

by JUSTIN DAUER

www.the-culturebook.com
@the_culturebook

Copyright © 2020 JUSTIN DAUER
Published by LEAD HAND BOOKS

Cover and book designer: JUSTIN DAUER
Cover illustrator: BOBBY PRICE
Book illustrators: BOBBY PRICE & MICHAEL GLASCOTT
Photographer: JUSTIN DAUER
Editor: ANN MAYNARD

ISBN: 978-1-733445023

Contents

Foreword

In Miranda July's 2005 film *Me and You and Everyone We Know*, the filmmaker invites us to see beauty and mystery in both the pedestrian and magical moments of ordinary life. Watching the film and encountering that vision changed me and how I move through the world. How marvelous, then, to pick up this book and discover that here, Justin Dauer is teaching us how and why we should be doing finding the beauty in the mundane ourselves. While July is a storyteller making art, Justin is a storyteller encouraging and advising you how to do your best work and how to help others do the same. As a storyteller, he fashions a sense of place, bringing to life not only his beloved Chicago, but people and locations from around the world.

Creative Culture: Human-Centered Interaction, Design, & Inspiration brings a courageous honesty to confront and address the uncomfortable truth that the workplace can sometimes be stressful, unfulfilling, and unhappy. If we can't acknowledge that, then we can't address it. And as Justin illustrates, a workplace that operates from a place of compassion is a workplace that is better for its humans but it's also a workplace that *produces better work*.

This book offers up even more Inception-style recursion: Justin reminds us that the values and principles we bring to our creative work (e.g., empathy and human-centeredness, for starters) should also be applied to our work culture, our work environments, and how we approach collaboration. Maybe your first response is "Well, of course!" but then if it's so obvious, why is it so rare? Why are phrases like "burnout" and "psychological safety" so common when we talk about work?

Once again, Justin points the way forward. Creating healthy and successful environments is the work of a manager. It's the work of a leader. But beyond title and role, an insight Justin offers here is that people working together are people first (and "creatives" or what-have-you, second). People are emotional and illogical, not time-and-motion output-generating units. Successful creative cultures not only acknowledge this but understand that this is a feature, not a bug. And these environments engage everyone in the tasks of fostering that work culture. Keep reading -- Justin will show you how!

Justin explains how to map out what a productive, effective, creative, and reflective day will look like. By engaging more closely with the ins and outs of one's daily life, a bit of mindfulness about the ordinary can deliver unexpected inspiration. Our creative brains can be engaged completely outside of a task to be solved. It's personally gratifying to see this particular exercise as it's identical to one that I've used in training workshops for years: we can be better user researchers by being better noticers.

Guided by Justin, a reflective practitioner with a passel of processes that you can benefit from, this book will help you move toward a healthier and more satisfying work life. That's something we all want, isn't it?

Steve Portigal
Principal, Portigal Consulting

For Owen, who completed a part of me
I didn't know existed.

Preface

In 2015 I had enough.

After nearly a dozen consecutive years in agency design leadership—and being privy (personally and second hand) to so many of the negative dynamics associated with that world—I wrote an article for *A List Apart* called "Resetting Agency Culture." The impetus for the piece was that there was a better way—a humble, people-first way—to treat employees, and one another. I had experienced this notion in practice, I had cultivated it personally, and I needed to broadcast those means from the mountain tops.

The article garnered near immediate, passionate feedback from people across multiple forms of media: web, print, television, radio, and so on. I understood these cultural issues were wider than the lens I had given them: it was less about the agency connection, and more about the *human* one. So in 2017 I released *Cultivating a Creative Culture*, painting upon a broader canvas: offering insight on finding a new best-fit role, up through someone's engaging first day in that role, to day-to-day empathetic interactions, and onward with longevity.

Since then, I've worked to evangelize this message (in tandem with actionable methods) as much as possible, appearing on a myriad of podcasts, co-hosting my own podcast, writing guest articles, speaking at events domestic and abroad, and filming a video workshop for e-learning firm MentorBox. Effectively every waking moment not co-parenting or working my day job (leading a shared-service department as VP of Human-Centered Design and Development) has been dedicated to this effort. Exhausting, but unquestionably worth it.

As a part of this journey, I've had the opportunity to engage in dialogues with many of you. For example, when I gave the opening keynote at the 2018 MidwestUX conference, I was also fortunate to sit in on "Presenter Office Hours" and have one-on-one conversations with attendees. I listened. I learned. The notion of being human-centered with one another at work resonated to such a degree that I hosted a second impromptu Office Hours the following day to get to everyone seeking to converse.

Copious dialogues like these over the past three years also confirmed an essential notion: design process often suffered from the identical themes that adversely impacted culture. Lack of human connection. Rushing. Exclusion. But as these plagues had a commonality, so did the best practices. I had only scratched the surface of this in the first book: the notion of being human-centered has an innate synergy between design process (and ultimate product) and office culture (and empathetic interactions). To the benefit of both dynamics, those touch points are identifiable and exploitable. Either way it's all about people.

And so I began to research. Observe. Interview. Write, revise, and write some more. During that time, my second son was born (*write, revise, change diapers, write, and change diapers some more). What began with the original book's theme became an organic and powerful evolution; less a dilution of focus, more the glue to the entire concept. That is why this book, *Creative Culture: Human-Centered Interaction, Design, & Inspiration* is as much a "first evolution" as it is the second edition of *Cultivating a Creative Culture*.

Introduction

It's Sunday evening. Another wonderful weekend is firmly under your belt. And yet, as you settle down into the couch, you're anything but content. There's that familiar feeling of dread in your stomach, uncomfortable and palpably inescapable. *Monday.* With the impending workweek looming large, events from the previous one replay in your head like an unwanted lowlight reel:

- The project review meeting in which your voice and feedback were disregarded entirely.
- The designs that were rushed to achieve a launch date at the expense of usability testing and human inclusion.
- The complete lack of energy and inspiration on your team, and from leadership, that ultimately compromised your end deliverable.
- The local half-day conference that you requested to attend, but were summarily denied. "You're needed in the office," after all.

The design field is largely composed of talented, creative and passionate individuals and yet all too often the organizational culture in which we're expected to work—*to create*—stifles the very gifts for which we were hired. When the fire within someone gets extinguished, more than just their best work gets lost; they may burn out, leave their company, or switch fields altogether. The potential impact on our industry is monumental. We as an industry are better than this—**and as human beings**, we deserve better too.

Whether you're in a leadership role wondering why your team seems miserable, or you're a passionate and dedicated designer dreading Monday, we can agree: a happy and well-supported employee is a fueled, charged, inspired creator. When a company gets their *creative* culture right, everyone's quality of work is elevated, quality of life gets strengthened, and the organization itself becomes organically championed by the very people it supports. Our team members deserve nothing less—no matter the size of the company, the industry focus, or their particular role. Those on the receiving end of the experiences we create deserve nothing less in kind.

As someone who's long worked with and supported designers and front-end developers in both design and tech-focused engagements, I've consistently seen how unhealthy internal cultures are tantamount to psychological abuse. How these environments have caused brilliant people to disengage from their crafts and question why they pursued their paths in the first place. I've seen how they've impacted *my* passions, *my* work, and *my* ability to thrive. And I decided to do something about it.

Designers and front-enders have a unique advantage in solving the cultural problems that are sucking the life out of us. Several advantages, in fact. The principles we will be discussing in this book derive from the perspectives and skill sets we already use daily: empathy, objectivity and, yes, ample creativity.

- Human-centered thinking drives our outward-facing work (user advocacy, usability, accessibility, the list goes on), so we will explore what happens when we turn that lens inward to address how to build trust and support.
- We cannot preach outwardly about empathy for those we're designing for if as designers, researchers, architects, developers (and on and on) we're not supporting each other. **The notion of being human-centered has an innate synergy between design process (and ultimate product) and office culture (and empathetic interactions).** We'll identify those touch points to ensure advocacy for people is omnipresent, and evergreen.
- To designers specifically (though I'm speaking to developers as well), visual communication and successful design are built upon rules toward end-product success. There is no room for subjectivity in critique and project evolution. We'll discuss what happens when a similarly unwavering standard is in place to uphold *humble* leadership and allow talented people the freedom to do what they do best, without sacrificing the bottom line.
- We share the ability to (and I'll hate myself in the morning

for using this term) "think outside the box" creatively: programmatically, or visually. It is our default setting, and it can propel us to seek out alternative forms of inspiration, or be amicable to adjusting our routines with the right tools. We'll be identifying those tools and how to implement them later in this book.

Creative cultures contribute to the resounding success of an organization and the work its team creates. They permeate the interactions at our office, the meetings we attend, and the manner in which we produce. *Creative Culture: Human-Centered Interaction, Design, & Inspiration* is very much about staying focused on human beings—both those behind the products, and those whom the products we design will impact. Getting there represents a shift in thought as much as in procedure.

The good news is we all can get there. Of course, there's a journey to be had along the way to our destination.

I'm inviting you to join me.

1

From
Square
One

/ 6

We create human-centered interactions and experiences in our field. Empathetic purpose drives our every decision. "Is this workflow intuitive?" "Does the level of contrast meet accessibility guidelines?"

Mobile First? In reality, it's *humans* first. This same mentality, turned inward, forms the cornerstone of something amazing: a creative culture.

A creative culture isn't felt in a company's home page elevator pitch, nor is it in the mission statement tacked to the wall of every cube. It isn't manufactured through after-hours beers with the team. It certainly doesn't grow out of "Hawaiian Shirt Day."

As we will discuss in this book, a creative culture *is* an environment where people come first: in policy, in business decisions, in managerial approach, in software selection, in design process, and in product release. Its foundation is one of mutual respect, palpable and harnessed energy, and a complete commitment to its livelihood. And its impact directly translates to quality of work (no, I didn't misspell "quantity"), quality of life, and measurable performance.

A creative culture sets the tone for an employee the moment they arrive for work on their first day.

Stepping Through the Door

The first day a new hire steps into their role is the organization's biggest opportunity for employee investment: welcoming them as a human being, rather than as a "worker." The new hire's buy-in can hinge on whether they get treated like a passionate and driven individual or a paid ass in a seat—and they will be looking for cues throughout the day.

People feel vulnerable on their first day in a new role and a new company. Hell, in their first *month* there are all sorts of adjustments in play. The environment is foreign, the faces are fresh, and in large part, the way in which projects get tackled on the day-to-day has yet to be learned. A new-hire will pay attention, logging away each detail and internalizing how they feel at each step. That first morning will communicate the organization's culture loud and clear. Is the employee welcomed at the door? Are they given a tour and introduced around? Or are they left to fend for themselves, setting up their workstation in silence? No one wants to feel lost or unwelcome.

It's safe to say we've all experienced both ends of the reception spectrum on our previous first day(s) on the job, successful or otherwise. For example, at one company I previously worked with, I was put into a client deliverable within the first five minutes of

THE FIRST DAY A NEW HIRE
STEPS INTO THEIR ROLE IS
THE ORGANIZATION'S BIGGEST
OPPORTUNITY FOR EMPLOYEE
INVESTMENT: WELCOMING
THEM AS A HUMAN BEING,
RATHER THAN A "WORKER."

laying eyes on my desk. At another, my arrival was a surprise to everyone but the person who hired me. And that person didn't show until 2:00 PM.

Alternatively, when an organization has a system in place to welcome a new employee (and not just onboard them), there can be magic. Best of all, designers and developers are uniquely equipped for doing precisely that.

For a moment, let's consider why we create personas in user experience design: to simulate the goals, desires, and thought processes of an individual, so as to better understand how they would accomplish a set of tasks. What do they want? How do they feel as they're progressing through that workflow? So now let's translate that general methodology—putting ourselves in the shoes of others—over to our wide-eyed new-hire's Day One experience.

A person on their first day wants to feel welcomed.
Flowers left on their desk, along with a handwritten welcome note.

A new employee would like to have easy access to logistical knowledge.
On that same welcome note is a URL to a landing page of helpful information. Slack credentials, email set-up, upcoming events, a list of restaurants in the area, etc.

Placing ourselves in someone else's mindset comes back to the adage we learned in our formative years: **treat others how you'd like to be treated.** The Golden Rule will serve us well in this book and beyond. So as you walk through the new hire's user experience, ask yourself: Does it match the story our organization tells everyone else?

When Story Meets Reality

A company tells its brand story to connect to its users, to keep them engaged, and to build relationships. How the organization came to be. Why its employees are charged to come into the office daily. Why they offer the products or services they do. It's also safe to say this brand story was communicated to the new hire multiple times, from the job description to the interview to the offer that brought them across the office threshold.

Story meets reality the moment a new hire walks through the door on Day One. For a new employee, all the positive momentum of signing on the dotted line and the perceived thrill of doing inspired work can live or die upon what happens next.

Now, whether or not you're a fan of Apple, it can't be disputed that they're one of the most powerful and influential brands on planet Earth. Full disclosure: I am one of the world's foremost Apple fanboys (it's a self-proclaimed title). So I was quite intrigued to learn how they infuse their brand into a new employee's Day One experience. Taking place "always on a Monday," as Adam Lashinsky notes in his book *Inside Apple*, new employees are given a heap of branded welcome package merchandise, shiny new hardware, and a free lunch. As an outside observer: nothing too surprising there.

Lashinsky goes on to describe how a new employee is expected to connect their new Mac to the company network completely unassisted. By and large, if you've made it through the hiring process as an Apple advocate, it's assumed you have the chops to handle that tech hurdle yourself. Otherwise, the intent is to get you to connect with other employees organically and establish a dialogue.

Lastly, "an informal 'iBuddy' system provides the name of a peer outside the primary team who can serve as a sounding board, someone for the bewildered new employee to ask questions," Lashinsky notes. In an organization with as many moving parts as Apple, it sounds like a great way to mitigate the feeling of being overwhelmed. Not casting a new hire into the sea of the unknown and acknowledging their humanity in the process is certainly a good approach.

From this fanboy's perspective, these elements align with the company's brand story: the individual over the machine, intuition meeting expertise, refinement meeting the unexpected, and so on.

But is that the best representation of the Apple culture? Hard to say with absolute certainty having not gone through the experience myself, but it seems like fairly standard corporate first-day fare, plus or minus an "i" prefix. Personally, what I'm looking for in a Day One is an experience that validates that I've made the right decision in signing the contract; one that propels me into my new role with positive energy and makes it crystal clear who my company is and what they stand for.

The New Day One

In the recent past, I found myself at a business whose culture was a poor fit on some very core principles: I felt unsupported (even exploited, a dehumanized resource), and the workplace lacked any semblance of a healthy, creative culture. It became clear to me that it was time for a change. And so, despite having no other role lined up, I left.

I dedicated the next few months to re-energizing, refocusing, and taking on some solo design and programmatic work. Over this time, I put a great deal of thought into how I saw my career evolving, considering a full gamut of options. I love crafting with my hands; perhaps carpentry? I thrive in environments where I can help grow the talents of others; maybe teaching? My alma mater, The School of the Art Institute of Chicago, was a walkable distance from my neighborhood. Effectively, I was drilling down to the core of what my passions were, and where I could harness the most creative energy and utilize it for the long term.

The core commonality from those ideas was a love for building things and surrounding myself with passionate brilliance. As the common thread throughout my career, that bloodshot tunnel vision ultimately led to a wonderful opportunity: building a design practice and creative culture from the ground up.

At Nansen, a Stockholm-founded digital agency, I was hired and welcomed by Swedish speaker, designer, and co-author of *State of Mind At Work*, Jaan Orvet. Our thoughts, approach, and mindset toward cultivating creative culture aligned in absolute perfect harmony. I'll be referencing his thoughts and our conversations throughout this book.

It was here at the fledgling Chicago branch of the company, upon a baseline of imported Swedish culture and egalitarianism supporting my every move, where the purest form of The New Day One was crafted. This cultural mindset derives straight from the Scandinavian concept of *Jantelagen* (or *The Law of Jante*), which effectively means that no one person is greater than anyone else. Having visited Sweden numerous times over the years, I've seen the success of the concept applied in a business setting. Moreover, humility and restraint saturate the culture of the entire country. It's a simple, human-centric viewpoint that has influenced the ideas in this book tremendously.

First Impression

Why do I care so much about an employee's first day when, in reality, it's a micro-fraction of their entire career? The fact of the matter is this: the consideration a company gives to how an employee is welcomed and brought into the fold speaks volumes as to what lies ahead.

After the ink is dry and logistics have been discussed, I arrange with our new team member to start with us on a Friday. As with the Apple example, many of us have likely become accustomed to first day Monday's; the prevailing thought being that consistency and momentum are inherent in a consecutive five-day workweek. And there is. That said, I'm looking for a different kind of momentum: one that's predicated upon time for reflection, which only carrying through the weekend will supply.

What follows is a process that's as finely tuned as it is organic. There are no client deliverables or billable work on tap today. Instead, I've laid out a series of events designed to acclimate my new team member as a valued human being, brimming with ideas and creativity. Through **acclimation**, **conversation**, **inspiration**, and **reflection**, their Day One unfolds as follows:

THE FACT OF THE MATTER IS
THIS: THE CONSIDERATION A
COMPANY GIVES TO HOW AN
EMPLOYEE IS WELCOMED AND
BROUGHT INTO THE FOLD
SPEAKS VOLUMES AS TO
WHAT LIES AHEAD.

Acclimation

The remainder of the first half of the day is setup and prep, both tangibly and perceptually. To the former, personalizing and configuring their laptop as they see fit, and working with the appropriate team members to secure licenses and install the tools they need. Instead of operating out of a closed-door office or sitting leagues away, I'm seated at the same table as my team. Any questions that arise will come to all of us:

> *"What are we using for file archival?"*
> *– Let me walk you through how we set that up.*
>
> *"Are we using Git or TFS for source code management?"*
> *– Our Front-End Lead, sitting right there, can best field that one.*

And a dialogue has begun.

We'll take a look at the office space and see how others are currently working and utilizing the environment. On the couches, in the kitchen area, at a coffee shop—nothing is off the table; it's about wherever you can do your best work. There's respect for the employee's process, and Orwellian eyes are not marking when people are walking out the door. It can take a few weeks (and maybe a brain cleansing) to erase a previous company's thought shackles from their minds, but this is how we operate.

Conversation

Up to this point, the Day One fare has been relatively straightforward. Our new hire has been acclimated with the team, the office space, and their workstation. Around noon I ask them to start winding down what they're doing, as it's time to head out for an off-site lunch. We won't be returning to the office today. The reactions I receive when I ask our new team member to pack up their things for the day range from a raised eyebrow to curious laughter.

Being ever mindful of a new employee's mindset on this first day, I ensure there's no logistical fumbling on the company's part: we head to a pre-selected, vetted restaurant. Over lunch, there's normal, human conversation. We've chatted a bit over the interview process, but now it's about getting to know this person as, well, a person.

"Hope you like this restaurant, it's one of my favorite places."

"Are you from the area originally?"

"Cubs or Sox?" (I don't care either way, but it's what Chicagoans ask one another).

Since the conversation evolves over bites of food, let's keep it casual but focused on genuinely listening. Taking a team member out to lunch on their first day isn't rocket science; how they're engaged (constructive dialogue versus cell phone tunnel vision) is where we see the most value.

The end of the meal doesn't conclude our conversation, however. After lunch, I'll have a café on tap (FIG 1) that's conducive to having a seat, quiet enough for hearing one another speak, and serves up great coffee (a good pour will be another running theme in this book). This environment informs a more passionate discussion: on development, on design, on inspiration, how our team functions within the organization, and current and future projects. The clock isn't watched, judging gazes aren't cast, and implications of seniority or hierarchy are left off the table. It's a small piece of the day, but the approach represents the creative culture they'll soon be thriving in.

The "inspiration" part of the discussion is no accident, either. It fuels the next part of our Day One.

Inspiration

With our bellies full and caffeine in our veins, there's only one

Fig 1: Pickwick Coffee Roasting, Chicago.

more expectation for the day.

"What inspires you in the city?" I'll ask.

The designer or developer's role is contextualized by digital endeavors. However, inspiration has no such limitations. As such, this isn't merely another conversation point: we'll physically go to wherever/whatever their answer yields. The Agora sculpture in Grant Park (Fig 1.1), the Tiffany Dome in the Chicago Cultural Center, and a craggy meditative stretch of Lane Beach in Edgewater (just north of downtown) have been some responses. My expectation, then, is to have them talk me through why [whatever it is] has inspired them. Our conversation offers me insight into their approach to visual or programmatic communication that transcends what folio work can yield.

The jaunt is more than a field trip, of course; it's a direct manifestation of the creative culture. This part of Day One can require some thoughtful guidance on behalf of the person driving the experience. It's a safe guess that this is like nothing the new employee has encountered before as part of their introductory experience, and opening their mind "on the spot" can be no small feat. In reality, their choice can be as simple as a stretch of road. Or a vinyl toy shop. Or a view of the city. If they get "stuck," we're not going to shrug and call it a day; I'll have some pre-selected inspiration spots ready to go, just in case.

In some instances, I've taken designers and front-end developers to the Modern Wing at the Art Institute of Chicago to appreciate and discuss a broad swath of creative inspiration. Design and code are art, and analyzing another artist's communicative process in their gallery pieces is mutual fuel. By having me provide the venue for inspiration, a different, though no less engaging, dialogue and critique have evolved.

Reflection

At this point, a first day brimming with copious amounts of healthy discussion (and coffee, and walking) has established a tone of humanized dialogue and mutual respect. Again, direct representations of the creative culture they've signed up for. Their Day One has come to its conclusion.

By the business clock there's typically not much time remaining; as such, our new hires can take the remainder of the day and weekend for thought and reflection on what was, very likely, a first day unlike any other they've had before. In fact, it hasn't been uncommon for hugs, or even tears (the joyous kind), to turn up as we part ways. That is the exact momentum I want to be carried through a couple of days of rest and into Day Two the following Monday.

The new employee now goes into their weekend with a crystal clear sense of how I, and the company, value and respect them. How we appreciate that they trust us to support their passions and abilities from Day Two onward. You can't fake sincerity or human decency, two fundamentals that many companies are incapable of supplying.

Though I've crafted this onboarding experience through the lens of my team, I've worked with the other members of management to ensure it's been translated and applied to how we hire within all roles at all levels of the company. Just as other departments are unique – and their respective leaders need to provide input on the actual implementation of this New Day One – other departments within other companies are of course unique, too.

To that end, I've seen encouraging adoption of this human-centered way of welcoming a new team member elsewhere. For example, I recently had a conversation with Chris Bolton from Portland, Oregon-based agency Murmur Creative on The Creative Agency Podcast #36. He cited that his agency had begun adopting the New Day One:

> *"When we hired our most recent person we created a card for them, we set up their computer, and rather than just dumping them into workflow, we set up a series of orientation meetings with different people in the office. And we sort of did that for like two days before we got into the day-to-day stuff ... we were realizing that was a really important place to start with a new employee. And I think that it felt good, and I think that hopefully we can keep developing that process with each new hire."*

FIG 1.1: AGORA SCULPTURE, GRANT PARK, CHICAGO.

I pressed for more information, asking if it felt natural to welcome someone in this way. Chris offered more candor:

"I think we all felt good about it. I felt like we were doing the right thing. It is funny because when you hire someone and everything's busy and you say 'ok, everything's a mess, I'll talk to you in fifteen minutes when I have a chance,' that doesn't necessarily feel all that unnatural either. Because sometimes you have a really busy workplace. Like it seems crazy to dedicate time to something like onboarding because there's so many things in the air.

But you also forget what an impression that makes on the person who is coming in, who's like 'oh, obviously I'm not the priority, I'm just like a cog in the works that will be attended to when someone has time.'"

Putting ourselves in the shoes of our colleagues, our users—hell, our fellow human-beings—is a notion that will always bring us to a valuable place.

Everyone Has a Seat at the Table

Value and respect—a human-centered approach has these ideals bound to the double helix of its DNA. It takes the first-day occasion leagues deeper than lunch and a handshake by providing an experience that is directly personal over boilerplate. Everyone in the office should be afforded the same thoughtful experience, as roles and seniority do not define the individual behind them.

Orvet speaks through the lens of Swedish culture when he cites precisely such a standard:

"It's ok to be a human; it's ok to be you. And on top of that, you can also be this role at the company where we work. It's always having the individual at the forefront."

It's a matter of planning to make sure a team member's

Day One is not just an uplifting experience, but also keenly representative of a truly creative culture. It's a matter of consistency and authenticity to make sure this carries through every single day-onward, organically.

Whether you're a designer or developer, client-side or service-side, internal or consultant, a baseline of intrinsic human decency, support, and talent development has to be established. Though this is a book written for designers and developers, these principles will lay the foundation for a healthy, supportive culture in any industry. As in design and development, those who are "doing it right" culturally are beacons whose example we'd do well to explore further. In fact, that's where we'll go next.

CHAPTER

2

A
Healthy
Dynamic

/ 6

Let me tell you about Nick Sarillo, a pizzeria owner.

A fellow lifelong Chicagoan, Nick is the founder and owner of two aptly named restaurants, Nick's Pizza & Pub, both situated in the city's suburbs. He's the author of *A Slice of the Pie: How to Build a Big Little Business*. He's also been featured in *The New York Times, Inc. Magazine, FastCompany, The Economist,* and a dozen other publications. And, he's a TEDx speaker.

In fact, I could expound endlessly upon where Nick's been featured and the media attention he's received, but the beautiful thing at the source is *why* he's received so much exposure. This humble yet brilliant man has developed a system of belief, support, and development dubbed "trust and track," which is the core of his business' culture and operations. What this means is that he gives his team the tools to succeed and to help the business thrive, and then trusts them completely to do exactly that. In large part, Nick is putting his near twenty-year-old multi-million dollar business' operations in the hands of local high school students. And they knock it out of the park, day in and day out.

Transparency and organizational flatness saturate every aspect of the business' culture and operations and form its foundation. In a tour of his Elgin location, Nick took me to the lower level of the facility where the company's full financial statements are tacked to the wall for all to see, updated daily. Everyone's current hourly wage is also listed on a whiteboard, and for those who haven't reached the salary level of their peers, the means to do so are listed on the same board. If you want to make more money, you train in more areas of the restaurant's operations. Nick and his leadership team will happily support your efforts.

Employees are entrusted with developing individual units of the restaurant's operations and P&L—the bar, the restaurant floor, etc.—including forecasting and inventory management. The employees become so advanced at their craft that Nick's internal training program, Nick's University, has been made available to the public. Fortune 500 companies have sent C-level staff to attend the courses, which in actuality may be taught by a seventeen-year-old high school student.

Underpinning all of this is the culture of the restaurant; it's quite literally built into the walls. As Nick led me around, pointing out some areas of the facility he built with his own two hands (Fig 2), every member of the staff was on a first-name basis with him. And he knew everyone's first name in kind. I witnessed a symphony of team members operating in harmony, swiftly preparing different areas of service for the evening rush.

"We don't have a lot of rules. We're not commanding and controlling. We're actually saying, 'make your own decisions,'" he told me over a slice of pizza. "Why I'm passionate about getting this word out there—and how we can create great places to work

FIG 2: A SMALL SECTION OF THE INTERIOR OF NICK'S PIZZA & PUB, ELGIN, IL.

in any organization—is I felt here I'm doing it in the restaurant business, which is typically thought of as a pass-through industry."

Trust in an employee, respect for their individual voice and support toward their growth are commendable core cultural qualities. Nick's team is charged and energized to come into work on a daily basis because the cultural match from the company's values (posted on a sign right in the lobby) to the individual's values is an exact fit. Openly shared and discussed during their interview process, those mutual passions and beliefs palpably carry through every day the employee walks through the door.

If there is one thing that Nick's example makes clear, it's that a culture of support, collaboration, and humility starts at the top. Nick Sarillo himself embodies those traits in every staff interaction, every communication put out to the team, and every leader he empowers to champion his business' values in kind.

The Transition of Fulfillment

Employees at Nick's Pizza & Pub are given the support to succeed and thrive from the day they join the company and as they move up through its ranks. And when a team member's role evolves to be inclusive of managing others, Nick's University has fully prepared them for that privilege.

A creative culture depends on humble, supportive leadership, and similar preparation for budding managers is equally imperative to ensure a healthy dynamic—not only between a leader and their team but also between a leader and their own sense of fulfillment.

Allow me to go Biblical for a moment:

In the beginning you went to school to match a curriculum to your passions. You deconstructed, merged theory with approach, and created layout from nothingness. And you saw it was good.

And you said, "I'll continue this journey professionally." With a career and a company Mac you designed and problem solved visually, leveraging your studies, intellect, and natural ability. You had a deep-seated need to create with your hands that had to be fulfilled. And it was so.

And you said, "I want to continue to grow." Over time and from role-to-role there was an evolution both within, and in organizational seniority: junior-to-mid, mid-to-senior, senior-to-management. Now with a team of your own, a responsibility toward the growth of others began to comprise the majority of your time and energy.

And it felt...strange. It felt different.

An Evolution

When a parent welcomes their first child, there comes a moment of stark clarity: it's no longer all about you. Though your own needs still must be tended to and respected, reward will now also be distinctly—*vitally*—obtained through the growth and development of another. As that notion applies to your vocation, this realization is a personal, and career, milestone.

How does a painter transition to a gallery owner / curator and remain fulfilled?

When I was a fledgling manager, I noticed I had developed a gradual sense of emptiness. I would come home from a day's work feeling unfulfilled. My days had become less inclusive of hands-on design the more I built out the team. I tremendously enjoyed, and valued, working with them to strengthen their work and provide a phenomenal creative culture in we could all thrive. But my mind hadn't yet made the switch to letting go of hands-on design and refocusing my sense of creative reward. Always one to have a personal design project (or three) going, I found my "creative thirst" was still primarily being satiated through those after-hours initiatives.

How does a lead guitarist transition to a producer and remain fulfilled?

All of this is a natural reaction, following years of personal identity and fulfillment that had been directly associated with hands-on design work. The fifth stage of grief in the Kübler-Ross model is acceptance; effectively embracing and owning the future. While "grief" isn't the exact relational concept for what we're talking about here, the recognition and respect of your career's evolution is a more apt thematic takeaway. It may ultimately be inclusive of a eureka moment, but is actually a gradual shift in practice.

A Commonality

Industry-agnostic, a Gallup poll from 2014 cited that 55% of workers in the U.S. obtain their sense of identity through their job. That's over half of the 6.5 million people employed in the tech industry alone who would likely associate self-image with their role.

In a previous position of mine, a team member who had recently ascended to management level and I would go out for regular coffee breaks to touch base. Topics varied from how supported they were feeling in their responsibilities (by me), how their team's energy was doing, whether they had any issues to cite, etc.

A brilliant and passionate developer themselves, this person noted one afternoon chat that they realized they were coding less and less. It was something they genuinely enjoyed doing, and they valued the sense of reward the came with programmatic problem solving. But they were feeling a bit thrown off by losing that part of their day (and self).

I began to set their expectations moving forward:

"With each person you hire, anticipate your direct involvement in hands-on development to continue to decrease by at least 25%."

In the moment, the percentage was fairly arbitrary; the notion that a transition was already in progress, and would continue toward a totality was the point.

We talked through the transition of fulfillment; how a sense of career reward ultimately evolves from being a hands-on creator to a facilitator and a teacher, and via imparting guidance from experience. And it is immensely rewarding—and an equally massive responsibility—to help foster and grow the passions of others. Once you realize the gift your career has yielded you, your sense of fulfillment will in fact be amplified.

An Honor

Designer or developer, it's important to never lose the part of yourself that craves hands-on creative problem solving. In the office, a leader who "isn't afraid to get their hands dirty" is a valued (and valuable) one. If time and responsibilities sometimes afford doing good work in that capacity, seize it. And if that's not realistic, personal creative outlets are always available. Evolving to the role of mentor and having your hands in motion needn't be mutually exclusive.

How does a painter transition to a gallery owner / curator and remain fulfilled?
By discovering other talented artists, promoting their work, and supporting their journey. **And by still painting.**

How does a lead guitarist transition to a producer and remain fulfilled?
By leveraging a career's worth of experience in the studio to help other musicians achieve their vision. **And by still playing.**

In the end, at the office it's about embracing a career's evolution and seeing it as an *honor* to support your team's passion for their craft. And it's about owning your responsibility to their successful output, leveraging your experience to their creative advantage and the betterment of the work you're all producing.
Humbly.

No Place for Pride

Pizza parlor or Fortune 500 tech juggernaut, the cultural backbone of a business will falter unless it's built upon respect. It's a simple notion: put the employees, the very talent keeping the lights on, first.
Hand in hand with that understanding comes leveraging the power of humility.

I Bet You Think This Section is About You

The weight with which unhealthy relationship synergies can, and will, undermine team members' collective confidence is massive. A lack of constructive mentorship and supportive guidance, or leaders who elevate themselves above those whose skill sets they should be cultivating—these things are as poisonous as open hostility.

It comes down to a single core issue: ego.

Ego is the antithesis of humility. Humility is essential to a healthy creative culture, and ultimately doing our best work. Why? Effective visual communication, intuitive experience design, and functionally engaging front-end development are not subjective. When there are clear project goals to be reached and problems to be solved, there is no room for ego.

When we make ourselves openly available to constructive feedback, we are doing our part to contribute to the ultimate betterment of a piece of work. By checking our egos at the door, we're innately operating in unison instead of hierarchical cliques. I cannot say this more emphatically: **It's good to be humbled.** Being surrounded by incredible talent and immersed in the brilliance of your team is a distinct gift, not a check on your own self-esteem.

In *Egonomics*, David Marcum and Steven Smith note the "cost of ego" on workplace culture:

- *Hearing, but not listening*
- *People thinking "me first, company second"*
- *Only the "right" people have good ideas*
- *Pressure to fit in*
- *Failure to challenge status quo*
- *Candid discussion saved for outside the meeting*
- *Failures being buried and never mentioned again*
- *Silos created and tolerated*
- *Meetings going longer than necessary*
- *Fear of making mistakes or admitting them*

HUMILITY IS ESSENTIAL TO A
HEALTHY CREATIVE CULTURE,
AND ULTIMATELY DOING OUR
BEST WORK. WHY? EFFECTIVE
VISUAL COMMUNICATION,
INTUITIVE EXPERIENCE DESIGN,
AND FUNCTIONALLY ENGAGING
FRONT-END DEVELOPMENT
ARE NOT SUBJECTIVE.

These erosions effectively permeate all office interactions and dynamics: human-centered and project-focused. In a survey for *Egonomics*, Marcum and Smith cited that 63 percent of employees say ego negatively impacts work performance on an hourly or daily basis.

Companies aren't successful based on the initiatives of a single person, humble or otherwise. It takes a motivated, engaged, supported team to help elevate the business.

Psychologist Dr. Maynard Brusman notes in his piece "The Costs of Ego":

"The hardest side of business to master is the human component. Entire industries are now dedicated to providing training and development to organizations challenged by the behavior of their 'human capital.'"

Ego needs to be self-managed, and also noted and corrected as it rears its ugly head. This self-monitoring has to happen daily, in every meeting and every conversation. It's evolution, with the goal being nothing short of crafting the best work possible within the healthiest environment imaginable.

For those in leadership, humility is a quality of paramount importance.

It's effectively impossible for an employee to respect a manager who puts their ego first. The "because I said so" approach our parents may have imbued us with growing up will now only serve to alienate (or piss off) others. It's the same as when a team or organizational leader "puts their boss hat on" in a dialogue; they can leave the hat on the rack by communicating consistently and clearly. If a team or practice lead is truly operating in your— and the project's—best interest, they'll, in fact, welcome the constructive criticism.

True respect levels the playing field culturally; everyone's voice is valued and an integral slice of the pie. By thinking, working, or communicating in a manner where we're putting ourselves over our teammates, we're immediately marginalizing them as human beings. We're discounting their abilities, ideas, and voice. Respect and collaboration are best friends.

Everyone in a company should have a seat at the table. Jaan Orvet and I chatted about this mindset over coffee while I was writing this book. As he noted:

"To Swedes that comes very easily because it's tied to the whole idea that anyone can share thoughts or ideas. Anyone can collaborate in any process. It doesn't matter how senior or junior you are. It has to do with a bunch of humans coming together to do something, and no human is worth more than another."

Jantelagen.

Successful leadership respectfully guides, augments, supports, and facilitates. I think we've all experienced examples of those who have faltered in that capacity. In a junior role I occupied eons ago, the culture was openly hostile toward mistakes and subjective failure. Whenever I was given the opportunity to present my work to a client, leadership's attitude was one of baited anticipation of any slips I might make (perceived or factual). After wrapping things up, I knew it was a toss-up as to whether management would simply leave the room without ceremony (the best case scenario), or if I'd get pulled into any of a handful of Herman Miller-furnished offices for denigration. This type of "leadership" behavior induces anxiety, inhibits confidence, and is tantamount to psychological abuse. No amount of employee compensation validates flaunting your own insecurity. This experience, on repeat, lead to handing in my notice. As Marcus Buckingham notes in *First, Break All the Rules: What the World's Greatest Managers Do Differently*:

"People leave managers, not companies."

Presenting work should always be an opportunity for employees to thrive and succeed. To that end, before any client-facing walkthrough of a project, I give my team some initial thoughts on what we should be covering: "Don't assume the client knows what we know, why we did what we did and what the benefit is to the user and the project's goals." And I clarify our presentation roles:

"I'll set the presentation up, and will chime in during your walk-through to supplement your dialogue."

If a team member has a bit less experience and hasn't presented their work before, they need the chance when they feel they are ready. It can start small. On completion, the team can have an open conversation to recap what went well and what needs improvement. If your supervisor isn't putting this together, you and your team most certainly can, very informally. The dialogue here is formed by feedback, not belittlement and threats.

The ultimate goal is exposing everyone to the process of talking through their work and giving them a (well-supported) chance. Whether in a presentation setting, a code review, or putting design work up on the wall for constructive critique, it's moving toward the same end goal. As team leaders or teammates, we need to support one another in honing our respective crafts. Beyond the betterment of one another and the project at large, this organically generates respect and positivity amongst all involved.

Providing and fostering an environment for open creativity and dialogue is valuable beyond measure: to the overall business, as well as the human-centered energy of the office space. We need to value conversation over oration, collaboration over delegation. People are hired to perform based on their experience and abilities, and acting as a barricade in any capacity is an endless loop of mutually lost opportunity.

Creativity and Ego Cannot Go Together

Jeong Kwan is a Zen Buddhist nun who prepares vegan meals for her community in a temple south of Seoul Korea. Chefs from some of the finest restaurants in the world make a pilgrimage to the Korean hinterland simply to taste, and be inspired by, her creations.

Is this because of her flatware line at retail outlets? No.

Is it because of her farm-to-table restaurant on the Vegas strip? Nope.

The ingredients from Kwan's dishes are culled from her own

un-fenced garden on temple grounds, which she affectionately calls her "playground." She has an intimate knowledge of, and connection with, everything that grows within. And it's this same connection that fuels a symphony she creates for the palate without the use of meat, dairy, or even some vegetables as staple as onions. The preparation process of her condiments (soy sauce, bean paste, chili paste) is unrushed, evolving over the time it needs—sometimes for *years*—so as to be instrumental in Kwan's mission to spread dharma through her cooking.

In Kwan's feature episode on Netflix's *Chef's Table*, she says:

"Creativity and ego cannot go together. If you free yourself from the comparing and jealous mind, your creativity opens up endlessly. Just as water springs from a fountain, creativity springs from every moment. You must not be your own obstacle. You must not be owned by the environment you are in. You must own the environment, the phenomenal world around you. You must be able to move in and out of your mind. This is being free. There is no way you can't open up your creativity. There is no ego to speak of. That is my belief."

Creativity and ego cannot go together; that's such a beautiful, clarifying statement. Kwan's process and the genius of her cooking are predicated upon connection and humility. We, as creators ourselves—code, design, product—can learn directly from her example.

Ego has no place in our processes and interactions. Furthermore, the people we're creating for must sit at the center of it all. Agnostic of accolades, the tools we're using, or devoid of rushed procedure, the humble connection with those on the receiving end of what we're producing, and with those *doing* the producing, is imperative to delivering unbridled quality.

Getting out of the Way

Let's think about how user empathy and advocacy are intrinsic to creating optimal user interactions.

Hand in hand with that understanding comes leveraging the power of humility.

No matter how much knowledge we have accrued and our depth of experience over various projects, we cannot impose a solution on a client simply because we feel it's correct: the user is always right. We test, we refine, we test again, all aimed at creating an organically perfected user experience.

As passionate craftspeople, we can guide and advise, being ever cognizant of how the user will best achieve their goals. Doing so makes for a better product. It's no ding in our fender to iterate, learn, and evolve. Just as we accept this fact—metaphorically stepping aside to allow user empathy to guide us—we must do the same for the skill sets and abilities of our team members.

We need to make ourselves open to letting our teammates do what they were hired to do. In short, we need to get the hell out of their way and let them shine.

What we find all too often in any business setting where designers and front-enders co-exist is that stakeholders at the team level, or higher in the seniority chain, can (and do) impose constraints throughout the process. Be it from a project's inception, or throughout its entire lifecycle. When there is too much ego in the room, there isn't much space left for creative pursuit.

So then, to our previous thoughts on humility: how does respect toward our team's talent (whether as their manager or their peer) cooperate with enforcing and directing how they should function? Project-wise, client communication-wise, or problem solving-wise?

It does not. Ever. Oil and vinegar, fire and ice, Batman and Joker.

The special sauce here is how project-focused interactions between teammates transpire. There is a fundamental difference between ordering ("It needs to be like this.") and guiding ("Your approach has bold thought behind it, but I wonder if it might be too strong; I'd consider this instead..."). The former is fed by ego, a singular mindset toward visual or programmatic communication. "You're wrong because I'm right." The latter response is predicated

WHEN THERE IS TOO MUCH
EGO IN THE ROOM, THERE
ISN'T MUCH SPACE LEFT FOR
CREATIVE PURSUIT.

upon humility and serves to leverage alternative perspectives. "You're on the right track. What if we tried it this way?"

In terms of the day-to-day, this means not hovering over a teammate (or employee)'s shoulder. Being a victim of backseat directing is belittling and nerve wracking. Involvement-wise, it also means not completely abandoning teammates to flounder without guidance up until the last minute, or at all. There are shades of grey on the spectrum of interaction between smothering and detachment.

Casual check-ins and informal dialogues throughout the day will humanize the experience, giving you the opportunity to talk through any current hang-ups or concerns. A successful dialogue is an open exchange of ideas. It's also a validation of approaches against a project's goals and a user's expectations. Being respectful of an employee's thought processes doesn't mean you shouldn't challenge them, however. It's organic coaching, transparent and respectfully delivered.

In Practice, From England

Some organizations excel at getting out of the way of their talent, and they are extremely passionate about it. Andy Budd and his business partners founded the studio Clearleft in Brighton, England in 2005. As he told me, they formed the agency to be *"the kind of place where, if we were employees, we'd like to come into work. But also, to get the right people, we wanted to have a great space."*

Over the years, their human-centered initiatives have consistently set them apart as beacons of creative culture. For example, in creating the Open Device Lab concept, allowing colleagues and the public at large into their space to test their digital work on mobile devices. Or in developing Hack Farm, their offsite employee-centric re-energizing retreat.

Widely publicized, their business model and cultural values inherently draw in the right kind of talent: those who have similar values, and also are seeking a truly creative culture in which to do their best work. Clearleft employees have the autonomy to operate as not just a dynamic group, but also as proponents and champions of their own work and problem-solving. Andy notes:

"You see really talented designers, really talented developers, really talented UX people, being told, 'you have to do this, because we sold it to the client,' or, 'you can't do that, because we haven't sold it to the client,' or, 'you can't say what you think to the client, because we might lose the contract.'"

There are numerous potential cracks in the foundation of that dynamic. It's likely team members were not included or consulted in the project's inception stage. Hours, features, scope, and/or budget were probably communicated in exclusive conversations. Or, there are stakeholders in the project who are setting design or programmatic direction at their discretion, effectively relegating the brilliance of the team to a production unit. In essence, there are too many cooks in the kitchen, and none of them are the ones who will be making the meal. As Andy told me:

"You're hiring really smart people, and then you're taking away all the opportunity for them to apply those smarts to the problem."

When a designer's creativity has to first be filtered through micro-management or ego, the losses are summarily painful to consider. Team morale is nil; their passions are wasted. Their insights and varied approaches to problem-solving lost. Collective energy is depleted, the project's end goals are compromised, and the end user is lost in the mix of dysfunction.

"How about this crazy idea where we hire smart people, we get out of their way, and then we let them solve the problems," Andy said of his business' model. *"It sounds really simple, but you'd be amazed how few companies do it."*

From Business to Employee

A healthy dynamic between company and employee is established upon the same foundational elements as peer-to-peer, peer-to-team, and peer-to-supervisor. The scale of the interaction rises, but the core values all feel the same.

Within all levels of the seniority chain of any organization, there is a responsibility to support, champion, or engage with the culture so that it can thrive.

Of course, I'm not advocating that business leaders have blinders on toward the bottom line. Nor am I implying that they need to take the focus away from what their role requires. I'm just saying they need to get out of the way of the talented people on their team.

Leaders need to be supporting and enabling managers and team leads to propel and enrich the creative culture on the day-to-day; they in turn must support their employees to have the same level of impact. That responsibility carries throughout the organization, from those who sign the paychecks to those who make the coffee (which can be the same person, sometimes).

People want to come into work, they want to learn and tinker and discover away from the office, and then bring those discoveries and that energy right back into their work and the culture.

Within the office space itself—as in, the physical surroundings— the business' cultural support needs to manifest itself in a tangible way. It can be as simple as some couches set aside in a nook or two for quiet conversation or refocusing: a space that's organic for gathering away from desks, or a coffee machine with some chairs or stools so people can linger for a few minutes if they'd like.

Beware the Perk

Sometimes, a company culture will offer perks that also appear to be wonderful demonstrations of humanity: a quiet sensory depravation-like enclosure for catnaps! A paid service that will come and clean my home, so I don't have to worry about such bothersome tasks! Free cabs home if I'm at the office past 9 PM!

In many cases, these are just cultural Band-Aids, and in large part, they're designed to:

1. Make sure you're physically at work as much as possible, and
2. Reframe unhealthy employee expectations as corporate empathy.

Unfortunately, the "sweetness" of these types of perks and how they're marketed (both internally and externally) puts the focus on some very unhealthy behavior.

The thing is, the inherent problem with brilliant employees is that they're by definition, well, *not stupid*. People know when they're being pandered to, or duped, or when they need to put on their knee-high boots. In fact, the only thing worse than not being sincere at all is faking it.

There are some simple, genuine nods toward an open and healthy culture that can come from on high. In company meetings, it's a strong sign of openness and transparency when profits, goals, new business, and operational matters are shared. People like to know what's going on with the company they're supporting.

They also like to feel seen. Appreciated. A gesture toward balancing practical information and human-centered stories can be communicating, say, who's working on an interesting personal project on their own time. Who is giving a talk at a Meetup? Who made a breakthrough in their work earlier in the month? Who deserves a pat on the back for helping out a teammate? Who learned a new skill? How might they integrate that new ability into upcoming projects? Sharing in this way puts a "soul" to the faces you pass in the hallway or bump into at the coffee machine.

Going All In

A healthy dynamic at all levels of an organization forms the backbone of a creative culture. The physical and psychological environment is better equipped to fuel inspiration on a daily basis, and sees the profit in employee growth, not just via the almighty dollar.

This level of investment on behalf of the business means no half measures. Included within that support of employee growth comes a core mindset of how the value of an employee's time is measured.

CHAPTER

3

The
Value
of Time

/ 6

100% billability.

There's a broad notion in our industry that an employee's utilization needs to be at, or near, maximum (business) profitability at all times. It's not uncommon for designers and developers to spend their entire careers under this cultural Sword of Damocles. For those in service organizations, this can mean their merit is quantified by how many line items on their time sheet are client job codes.

This mentality sets the precedent that an employee's worth directly correlates to their tally of completed work. It also effectively crushes any opportunity to harness inspiration. No available time means no time to harness or grow energy; available time is micro-analyzed and frowned upon until it gets filled. It's a cancerous loop.

On the other side of the coin, profitability is not the sole driving factor behind why a company is created, why a project is taken on, or why an employee comes to work each day. Companies *can*, in fact, be "a good place to do good work." That's exactly how Clearleft was conceived and successfully continues to operate today. In fact, many businesses cross-industry are founded upon this humble yet amazing goal; they just lose their soul, and inspired employees, along the way.

To do our best work, to grow our skill sets, and to cultivate an environment in which passions thrive, we first need to stop casting a judgmental eye at "available" time that supports employee growth. We then need to ensure such time is planned for, available, and encouraged in practice.

Challenging the Basic Perception

Clearly, a business relies upon billable hours to function; that's what keeps the lights on. But allowing your employees the time to apply their efforts to other things is important too. There's naturally a balance to be had between securing time for employee development and leveraging it for project goals and deliverables. Some weeks and cycles will afford more time blocks than others. That said, much of the time we'll be discussing here is interlaced organically throughout a workday, instead of conglomerating in large "away from the desk" units. It's quality and usage versus quantity and waste.

What I'm advocating for represents a shift in thinking, a shift in process, and a shift in how we track and value employees' time. As an industry, we've made similar thought and procedural shifts in this capacity before—as in when we began advocating for the user at the discovery level, bringing UX into the forefront of our approaches. Today, it's exceedingly evident that time spent on discovery and UX is vital for a digital project's livelihood; we need to apply that same reevaluation to time spent on employee success.

It's a shift that comes at multiple levels, ultimately. Ownership needs to support and champion the value of growth-based time and empower managers to enforce the practice procedurally. Project managers and product owners need to ensure such time is consistently planned and allocated for in scheduling. It's one of those things that are easy to neglect ("If we could just put in a little more overtime this week to get ahead of the curve...") but those decisions ultimately form small cracks in the cultural foundation.

It can start in the smallest of ways: sitting at one's desk, reading an article on programmatic advancements. Hell, sometimes it's nice just to pause for a few moments and catch up on the news. It's less the act of what you're doing, and more about resetting your creative energy through a calm and predictable activity—without worrying about "getting caught."

Previously in my career, if I happened not to have a project file open when management walked by, it was a death sentence for my remaining workweek. "Clearly you don't have enough going on right now," I'd be told. The reality was I had plenty of work, but I wasn't doing my best problem-solving; I needed a "mind breather," and got summarily chastised for it. You'd walk around the office and see people leaning forward in their chairs trying to shield their screens in stolen moments of un-billability; each of us pitiful in our predicament and posture.

In what amounts to a fraction of a percent of someone's day, we need to communicate (verbally, procedurally, physically) that it's perfectly acceptable to, quite simply, pause. Refresh. Regenerate and renew. Management needs to trust their employees to seize these moments with sincerity and ensure they know they're allowed to do it in the first place.

For employees, especially newly hired ones, having such time made openly available can be a bit of a shock. It's as though we need to be de-brainwashed of what has been expected of us throughout our careers. Unhealthy professional relationships can

LET'S CALL IT "THE ACT OF THE LINGER." THAT SIMPLEST OF GESTURES—NOT RUSHING BACK TO YOUR DESK—IS ONE SMALL STEP FOR EMPLOYEE, ONE GIANT LEAP FOR CREATIVE CULTURE.

become our default setting, like a dysfunctional security blanket. It may be a challenging awakening, but it's one that yields a pretty butterfly post-metamorphosis.

"Is it ok that I'm sitting on the couch in the lobby right now reading an A List Apart piece?"

"This chat by the coffee machine on the new .js framework is really interesting; I wonder if it's ok to talk it through?"

"I'm having a problem-solving block for some reason today; think it's cool to go out for a walk and reset?"

The answer to all of the above questions comes from the immortal Heisenberg: You're goddamn right.

Designers and developers, it's your right to have time in your day-to-day for professional development, and it needn't come at the cost of putting food on the table. Being utilized solely as a line-item resource in an Excel spreadsheet is an insult to your passions, evolution, and ability to do your best work. Once we all recognize that we're human beings, the door is open for so many incredible things to happen.

In Organic Interactions

When you're part of a healthy creative culture where both project work and professional development carry equal weight, there are numerous ways in which to harness that energy. It all begins from seizing organic interactions throughout the day.

Let's call it *the act of the linger*. That simplest of gestures—not rushing back to your desk—is one small step for employee, one giant leap for creative culture.

Different office space configurations play their role in how and where organic interactions can present themselves. Sometimes a floor plan is less open, and cubicles or demi-partitioned desks comprise the lay of the land. Or, offices and doors form a physical, barrier, blocking that creative energy from being shared amongst everyone. Rearranging the room may not be an option, so interactions need to be consciously sought out. The responsibility is on everyone to make themselves available: physically by getting up out of their chairs and away from their desks, and mentally by engaging their teammates.

At the office, if I'm eating on premises, I'm not a long lunch kind of guy. It's a personal preference, not a cultural constraint. I'll have some reading material out next to my food, quickly clear my plate while perusing, and clean my place. It may not be the most visually elegant procedure (the crumbs in my beard and aghast coworkers tell the tale), but that's how I enjoy my lunch. Others around me enjoy at a slower pace, chatting and laughing with their friends and co-workers, and letting any negative energy or stress slough off—they are on break after all. Conversations range from current projects to the last episode of a TV show everyone is engrossed in, to an exhibition someone attended over the weekend. Sometimes the dialogue lasts a half hour, sometimes an hour plus. That's how they enjoy their lunch.

Throughout the day, I'll pause by the espresso machine and enjoy a cup. Slowing myself down, tamping grounds into the portafilter to get the right amount of crema; it's a meticulous detail-centric act that produces a tangible (delicious) result. The process calms and refocuses me, despite the fact that I'm by no means an ace barista. Sometimes, I'll have a stand-up with my team around the espresso machine, or ask those I bump into about their day. That's how I enjoy my coffee. Others will come into the kitchen, pop in a single-serve coffee pod, take a sip and head straight back to their chair. That is how they enjoy their coffee.

The point is that there's no right or wrong way to capitalize on those available moments. Different things work for different people throughout the day, but there is a definitive common thread no matter the use case: everyone is taking due time in these organic interactions to let the moment stand and let things unfold organically. In having the cultural opportunity to have such time available without fear, the possibilities for profession-based dialogue, eureka moments, and attacking problems freshly focused are endless. All the while, we're interacting as human beings, creating in an industry that is inherently human-focused.

In Planned Interactions

It's no concession toward a creative culture to have planned moments of interaction throughout the day, or week, to complement those that organically unfold. In fact, these calendar-secured blocks of time consistently keep the energy flowing. They're a boon. The secret sauce is ensuring such time is optimized for channeling that energy back into their work, and in keeping people mutually motivated.

For example, I run a weekly meeting internally dubbed "Creative Inspiration Wednesdays." It's uncoincidentally situated (US) morning mid-week and serves a very specific purpose. These mornings are intended to start a little bit slower, as the meeting begins at 9:30 AM; there's enough time for a longer breakfast, but not enough time to dive into client work. Again, no coincidence. Between offices from international branches, designers and developers dial in on-time to talk through things that have inspired them over the past seven days.

We share our laptop screens and elaborate on the bits of inspiration we want to share. Low hanging fruit in our industry is a thoughtful website design, or an interesting mobile app interaction, or a book or article someone read on a developing digital trend. Nuggets of inspiration that are directly relatable and applicable to what we're creating daily.

What really generates discussion though are the areas of inspiration that deviate from the digital realm. An online video clip of a documentary on graffiti. An illustrator's body of work. The design of a Bauhaus-inspired Max Bill timepiece (ok, that one was me). We talk through why these areas of inspiration away from the viewport mean something to us; the thought process, how they tackled a problem, or how something specific was achieved through its constraints.

This meeting can last anywhere from twenty minutes to an hour. As the ultimate stakeholder in design and front-end's deliverables in Chicago, I ensure the environment of the call is relaxed, unrushed, healthy, and productive. I'm fully cognizant of—and never lose sight toward—the client-centric work to be accomplished for the day. And so are the call's participants; everyone is fully capable of self-managing their workload to ensure they can have this time for inspiration. Following the call, one of our team members posts the links to a private board for everyone to be able to reference now and in the future.

Our client's work is imperative, of course. But each of us knows it's just as important to have the chance to recharge our energy with inspiration that's cross-medium, cross-culture (and in this instance, I mean between international offices and those in the US), and can be discussed and drawn upon as fuel throughout the remainder of the week.

This fuel serves as a consistent recharge for our creative energy, and in turn, helps the caliber of our work stay consistent. Fuel begets energy; energy begets quality.

The Art of the Fika

Standing "coffee dates," if you will, are also a great way to sync up throughout the day, away from our desks, and recalibrate ourselves. In Swedish culture, there is the concept of *fika*, which means to, more or less, take time out during the day for coffee and a bite to eat. However, it's much deeper than that: it's time to catch up with a friend, to interact as human beings. It's time reserved specifically for taking a break. Fika is such an important thing to Swedes, in fact, that it's often built into employee contracts.

Drift is a magazine that covers coffee culture globally. Their Stockholm edition aptly put it:

"Fika is the thread that weaves Swedish social customs together, and

it's the ultimate nod to the idea of slow living. In our fast-paced world, where we are constantly on deadline or planning our schedules around meetings and events, we crave opportunities to slow down. Swedes actually embrace those opportunities."

When I first observed fika a handful of years ago at the office, watching the Swedes around me get up mid-afternoon daily, stop working, and just...chat over coffee and pastries, I thought I was hallucinating. Are they just talking to one another in the middle of the day? Is that phone going to keep ringing? It took me a good week to allow myself to get up as well and join them; my previous experience as an employee in the US had psychologically shackled me to my chair.

The concept, in practice, is a revelation. Employees have their planned fikas, they meet at various spots in the office during the afternoon, and they take their due time to chat with one another. It's beautiful, it makes perfect sense, and I absolutely cannot imagine having it any other way. The rejuvenation and humanization of the interaction are inarticulable, their value immeasurable. It's a Swedish cultural staple, but any culture can seize its benefit.

In Open Areas

Some locations within an office can be organically conducive to employees congregating for a conversation. As we've discussed, the coffee machine, kitchen area, an employee lounge, all can fall into that bucket. There's also a tremendous benefit in designating an area for open thought and creation, without cannibalizing needed workspace.

First, there needs to be a critical delineation made as to what constitutes a space for harnessing and renewing energy. It comes down to the difference between a **distraction** and an **outlet**.

For example, when I was in the early stages of my career and came home from a challenging day at work, I'd turn on my video

FIG 3: TANGIBLE MEDIA CAN RESET OUR CREATIVE PROBLEM SOLVING.

game system and lay the smack down on pixel people in *Street Fighter* for a couple of hours. It'd ultimately be time for bed, yet I was still completely wired and carrying the same negative energy with me that I brought in the door. All I had done was distracted myself. Eventually, I learned that I needed to actually *do something* with that anxiety and stress after work: going for a run, building something, illustrating something, etc.—something healthy, something constructive, and something that afforded actual personal benefit.

Consider an area within the office that encourages employees to work with tangible media, completely out of the context of the digital realm. We're all problem solving during our day: visually, structurally, programmatically. There's immense value in refocusing that process back to making decisions, exploring, building, and experimenting with our hands. I'm not talking about scrimshawing a masterpiece out of a single piece of oak or chiseling a sculpture out of a block of Italian marble. No, I'm talking about Legos. Inkwells and brushes on 80 lb. paper (FIG 3).

CONSIDER AN AREA WITHIN
THE OFFICE THAT
ENCOURAGES EMPLOYEES TO
WORK WITH TANGIBLE
MEDIA, COMPLETELY OUT OF
THE CONTEXT OF THE
DIGITAL REALM.

3500-piece puzzles.

Jo Cofino's article "Why Lego's CEO Thinks More Grown-Ups Should Play at Work," asks the man behind the bricks, Jørgen Vig Knudstorp, about the value of hands-on play in the workplace. Citing that "one of the biggest mistakes companies can make is to think that sticking a foosball or Ping-Pong table in the office equates to playfulness," Knudstorp noted:

> *"It goes a lot deeper than that, and play offers a lot of promise for businesses. Creative companies create inspiring environments. Tim Brown of innovation and design company IDEO says play creates a risk-free environment that encourages people to experiment, as there is no such thing as failure. It is much more conducive to problem solving than the traditional 'I am right and you are wrong and there is only one way of doing things.'"*

Within an office, does it need to be a planned thing to approach this "play area" and create? It can be, but a developer may also just hop out of their chair, beeline it to the Legos, and start building something with intensity. Perhaps a coworker is there already, building and deconstructing. Some may prefer solitude in creation; others may question, collaborate, and refashion.

TED speaker and psychiatrist Dr. Stuart Brown cites the benefits of this type of motor skill-centric activity for adults in his aptly titled book, *Play.* Agnostic of role, career path, or skill set, he notes that it's more about the voluntary act itself instead of the outcome of the creation. Taking you "out of time," it affords a sense of engagement, augmenting problem solving and creativity.

In Areas Without Walls

For the cost of some art supplies or a trip to the toy aisle at Target, an organization can significantly augment its support of all time with tools for regenerating energy. There's an endless fountain of inspiration to be had away from the psychological container of a desk in a healthy creative culture.

But let's take it a step further and look beyond the confines of the workspace.

To only set our sights on our office space as the sole means of recharging and refueling is to ignore the entire world outside the front door. The personal (and business) value is found in how we leverage the energy obtained away from our desks and infuse it back into our work. A genuine creative culture supports drawing from both indoor and outdoor environments as needed.

4

Beyond
the
Viewport

/ 6

While our livelihoods exist within the digital realm, inspiration has no such contextual boundaries.

We've discussed outlets, interactions, and moments to be seized while in the physical walls of our work environment. Within those halls is an enormous amount of energy to be harnessed and channeled (via our people), but what of the environment we pass through as we make our way into the office (via the people we design *for*)?

In a design process, spatial dynamics are key to being mindful of the bigger picture in our work (via ethnography, user research, observation, etc.). Culturally, human connection and professional relationships are cultivated outside cubicle walls and email threads. In both instances, leveraging tangible interactions begins with the act of getting out of our chairs.

The Revolution of Stepping Away from Your Desk

There is an entire world of design and inspiration beyond the context the digital world affords us.

Though "thinking outside the box" is a hack term at this point, the sentiment is genuine: the box is our MacBook Pros. The soft ambient glow of a Retina display bathes our faces, its viewport locks our gaze and, in turn, our bodies. "Taking a break" often just means clicking over to a different screen. I'm sometimes guilty of this myself, and the process has a pattern:

- Visual design block hinders momentum.
- "Best of" collections populate a barrage of new browser tabs. This daily winner, that nominee.
- Via minimal effort I've ascertained mass audience-approved web fonts, grid patterns, and content integrations.
- It goes on: responsive navigational system libraries. App UI interaction snippets. All ripe for the picking. My synapses enjoy

their coffee break.

Having my viewport blinders on robs me of not just original thinking, but also truly understanding to where my inspiration vanished. Or where it came from in the first place. Quieting our minds is no small feat with the digital world perpetually clawing for our attention. Screens are omnipresent: at our desks, in our pockets, on public transport. It takes attention and effort to reserve time out of their reach, and exertion is always at odds with comfort—and habit, for that matter. Comfort is the bane of advancement.

There are smaller moments in the morning where I simply need to get outside. With the morning's calm, preceding the day's (and clients') awakening. Some days welcome us with inspiration waiting to be seized, to be channeled as fuel as project- centric minutes loom large. Sometimes inspiration requires you to seek it out.

It's at this moment where we need to challenge ourselves.

As with my earlier fika example of initially being "unable" to join my coworkers, this is the definitive point in which we liberate ourselves from those mental shackles. In the drudgery of the post-lunch afternoon, this can manifest in a simple walk around the block. The culture of the office sets the supportive tone here by letting these moments occur unfettered. In one company I worked at previously, I was required to sign out at the reception desk every time I walked out the front door; for lunch, for a breath of fresh air downstairs, for anything. The minutes I tallied, to be made up apples-for-apples upon my return. In this single act, I felt marginalized, scrutinized, and patronized. It provided for a steady stream of head-shaking resentment amongst my co-workers as well.

Trust and Performance

A creative culture openly supports the basic human need to let our minds breathe away from our desks. It lets the energy outside our walls inform the people within. There's demonstrated trust from company to employee in getting out of the way, leaving that door wide open, and not lording over their minutes like Sauron over Mordor. Of course, there's a balance to be had: an employee must also understand that this doesn't mean "take the afternoon off and go on a discovery walk"; something in the ballpark of a half-hour is usually solid. If people feel trusted, they will reward that notion with freshly charged creativity and increased productivity.

The study "Employee trust and workplace performance" published in the *Journal of Economic Behavior & Organization* conducted research on the relationship between employee trust and workplace performance across three variables:

1. The businesses' financial performance
2. Labor productivity
3. Quality of service or product

Across strict measurement criteria, they noted that, "higher levels of average employee trust in managers appear to be positively related to workplace financial performance and labor productivity." In terms of quality of service or product, "employee trust is positively associated with being in the 'a lot better than average' category." Put simply: employee trust in management directly translates to a high quality of work and company profit.

On the business' end, this trust and support need to be directly communicated to an employee when they're hired. If it comes "through the grapevine" or is passively observed from afar, the notion that they can just take a break outside might be perceived as suspect or only for a privileged few. Even in a culture that's known for its employee and growth-centered climate, this has to be an absolute known quantity from Day One.

Government Digital Services (GDS) in the UK, which specializes in "the digital transformation of the government," goes as far as to physically post on a wall a list of exactly what their employees can seize, culturally. The "unofficial stuff," as they've dubbed it. Noting things "it's ok to do," such as "go somewhere else to concentrate" or "not check email after hours," employees new and old are crystal clear on the wonderful, oft-unspoken, benefits their culture has to offer. Simple gesture, long-term impact.

On Foot

In the spirit of seizing cultural benefits, let me show you what I do when my inspiration is lacking. I'll draw my example from a morning I had not too long ago.

Heading out the front door as others walk in, I'm also exiting a state of stagnation. As I breathe in fresh air, I'm making myself available to an influx of new energy; I move, and I observe. Am I looking for something that will directly translate to the digital space? No. Perhaps the way a sign painter across the street painstakingly applies letterforms will influence my web typography, or the way a tree branch buckles under a landing bird will inform a web animation, but I'm not banking on it. In eureka moments, direct relations can happen. Such events are gifts, but the intent here is much broader.

Sensory interactions both grand and intimate are longing to be harnessed, processed as fuel. From my company's Chicago location on this morning, I ventured East with subconscious intent toward the Loop. Casting my gaze upward, architecture carved its place in the sky. Refocusing on the bustle before me, a commuter walking in quick step thoughtfully paused to lend directions to a tourist. "The First Time I Met the Blues" poured forth from a street musician's American Deluxe. Ingenuity, humility, and soul were the reward for my half-hour journey. Our human-centered jobs need to consistently be inspired by the very humans we're creating for.

The digital realm is seductive. As problem solvers—simply as users ourselves—we're ever drawn to its lure. Stepping away from "the box" is all it takes to begin a thought shift toward the value of out-of-office inspiration.

In Curated Environments

The inspiration we're able to cull from the world outside our office's front door is in large part "moment-specific," if you will: the interactions, observations, and experiences we happen upon can and will vary based on an endless degree of chance and circumstance. That spontaneity, and the variety it presents, is a large part of its value.

On the other side of the coin, visiting a thoughtfully curated environment where someone has keenly and specifically thought of every detail affords a different, tangible inspiration. One that's deliberately planned and innately consistent.

Our field requires we give empathetic thought to the implications of every decision we make. We're creating interactive experiences for humans that serve to be as functional, usable, and intuitive as possible. At the same time, we're considering the value of every detail and the role it plays in the quality of the end product. This is where the synergy of inspiration between the digital and physical realms functions to our advantage.

Beauty in the Details

The Soho House group has hospitality-focused properties spanning Europe and North America. Designed as a space for "creative souls" to inspire and be inspired, the brand is known for its thoughtful fusion of industrial design, elegance, and comfort in its décor, furnishings, and art. Letting the respective building's history and geographical location keenly inform the creative process, the painstaking craft of this marvelous balance is driven by resident Design Director Vicky Charles. As she noted in *Better Interiors:*

> *"Our design is very much led by and sympathetic to the local environment. We always work with custom design furniture and antiques but we respect the original finishes and architecture of the*

OUR FIELD REQUIRES WE
GIVE EMPATHETIC THOUGHT
TO THE IMPLICATIONS OF
EVERY DECISION WE MAKE.

space, so each property is different."

The Chicago House is walkable for me, and one I often frequent for haircuts, coffee, or writing (including the section you're reading right now). Not only is every property unique, but each room in every property also has no duplicate; spanning the 40 quarters in this building, that's a non-trivial feat. The structure—originally The Chicago Belting Factory—leverages much from its own history, as well as the city's past, toward its present incarnation.

The structurally unsound water tower on the building's roof was deconstructed and repurposed as a mural in the lobby. The blue tone employed on the exterior awnings, with full intention, matches original paint that was discovered in the warehouse. Chicago's last remaining tannery, Horween Leather, lent their craftsmanship to the gym's equipment.

Sitting on the Club Floor over a cup of coffee, there's an energy to the space that's fueled by these thoughtful details. They factor right down to the curve of the coffee cups and writing-conducive workspaces. These little unobtrusive rewards elicit positive emotional responses; they're complimenting my experience of writing or just defusing. As in my digital, experiential work, the very same positive emotional responses gained through thoughtful user interactions compliment my (user) journey.

To Caffeine and Beyond

It's no secret that people gravitate to coffee shops to work, read, or catch up with a friend. Like Soho House's Club Floor, many coffee shops afford what *The Atlantic's* Conor Friedersdorf calls, "just enough distraction." That is to say, enough noise to break the harsh silence of an office environment, but not at live concert levels. Cafés can make for a phenomenal alternative for doing charged work away from our desks, especially when the environment is a deliberate, curated space conducive to creative energy.

My team at work has full reign to design and code agnostic of workspace; around the office proper, that freedom is well-utilized.

There's still an apprehension to do so away from the office. So engrained are we to stay within our physical walls during business hours that I've actually had to make it a **requirement** that my team picks a café to work from one morning a week. Without having chatted about it beforehand, I later discovered Jaan Orvet did the same imposed coffee shop trip with his team over in Sweden. Psychological shackles of unhealthy cultures past have no geographic boundaries.

The selection of which coffee shop to work from isn't an arbitrary one. Via peer dialogues and online reviews we do our homework in advance, ascertaining how conducive a potential space is to curated inspiration and seizable energy. One such long-time favorite is Heritage Bicycles General Store, in Chicago's Lakeview neighborhood. Founded by Michael and Melissa Salvatore, Heritage is equal parts custom bike manufacturer (the first in the city since 1982) and ultra-curated café. In an open floor plan intentionally designed to generate energy and conversation via its seating arrangement (mostly communal), the "placement with purpose" interior decorating offers plenty of spatial inspiration.

The ol' typewriter, handcrafted reclaimed wood table, and coffee shop combo may scream "hipster," but for our intents and purposes that's an association I'm quite comfortable with. The hipster-driven "handcrafted" movement gets its share of sneers, but at its heart is a passion for craft: through coffee shops, niche clothing stores, or farm-to-table restaurants. In that way, be it through the lens of beans or selvedge denim or pork shoulder, there's a deliberate and focused nature that fuels the selection of elements down to a microscopic level of detail. Quality in the end product defines the goal of the process.

Over the years, via syncing up with Orvet in Stockholm for our standing coffee chats, we often continue our dialogue outside with specific stops in mind. Sometimes, it's been a denim boutique on the island of Södermalm. Other times, a brilliantly stocked magazine shop. One such example of the latter has been Papercut, who's ambition is "to create the ultimate store for people who consider fashion, art, literature, design, film, music, etc. an important part of their lives." Its scope and scale have been daunting to me in the times I've had the opportunity to browse.

That said, the sheer quantity of material has not come at the sake of its careful selection; the shop is magnificently curated. At the various companies with which Jaan has done his experience-based work, he's brought his team to Papercut, mid-workday, often. As he noted about one such excursion:

> *"The decision to go there was to spend an hour in a nicely curated environment where the people that work there can answer a question about any title. (It's about) being in an environment where someone has thought about every aspect, because that's what we need to do. So, instead of talking about the importance of quality, going to a quality place to pick up magazines is a way of bringing it into day-to-day life."*

Observation as Fuel

Colleagues have asked me, *"How do you workshop 'inspiration'?"*

All of the observation-centric inspiration we've discussed to this point – be it spontaneous or curated – has direct leverageable value toward the quality of our digital work. Training ourselves on how to document these moments to later be processed as fuel is where the magic begins.

About a year after the first edition of this book's release I was invited to speak in Stockholm, Sweden at international agency Futurice's "Design Day". Under the banner of "Rethink / Refresh", Futurice flew in designers from their six offices — Helsinki, Tampere, London, Berlin, Munich, and Stockholm — for a day of inspiration, collaboration, and recalibration. The event was conceived around the following mindset:

> *The meaning of design in digital services has long ago passed a tipping point. For one, design is no longer exclusively about digital or the visible — but that's not news. What is a bit on the newish side is a need for a different type of projects from our clients around the world.*

In addition to speaking on the methodologies *Cultivating a Creative Culture* to kick off the day's events (at 2:00 AM Chicago time, no less), running a workshop on harnessing and leveraging inspiration was my contribution to the afternoon program. As designers and researchers, we have an implicit requirement to observe the human beings we're creating for, connect with them, and engage them in our process and design. This very exercise can be run in the comfort of your own workspace to help your team train their eyes and develop some simple, effective observation-based habits.

As much as this was about the Futurice team training their eyes and minds, it was about the human connection; people sharing their stories and organic dialogue. This broke down barriers for many who didn't know one another previously, having arrived from different international cities and offices.

The Plan

Let's consider some points along a potential day's journey:

1. **Commuting** through the city on a given morning
2. **Pausing** for a cup at a favorite café
3. **Creating**, once in "design mode" at your desk

These experiences (1, 2) comprise a million moments waiting to be annexed as inspiration, and processed as fuel (3).

On a seven foot-long sheet of paper (Fɪɢ 4), let's map the above points (1, 2, and 3). By intent, this should preferably lay flat on a large table instead of being whiteboarded in dry erase marker (though the latter scenario will work in a pinch). I'll explain why I prefer the former method in a moment.

Beneath each experience we'll list a couple columns noting what people can **Observe (A)** at points along the way, and what the **Takeaways (B)** were from the respective observations. For example, under those sub-headers I use a couple pre-written kick-starting concepts:

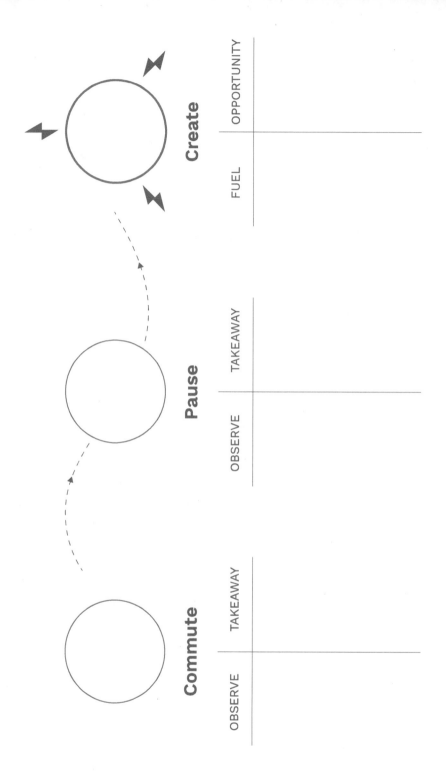

Fig 4: The Workshop Journey Map in its Default State.

FIG 4.1: "COMMUTE" IN LEGO FORM. FROM THE STOCKHOLM, SWEDEN WORKSHOP.

1. **Commuting in the city:**
   A. Seeing someone pause and give directions to stranger
   B. Empathy
   *This person has somewhere to be; they're pausing to help a stranger
   find where they need to go. This person has been in that stranger's shoes
   before and they understand how it feels to be lost.*

2. **Pausing in a café:**
   A. The act of crafting an espresso
   B. Process-to-quality
   *The barista is going through a very detailed process: tamping down
   the grounds, getting the pour and the crema just right. Preceding this
   was the careful selection of the roast. Ultimately, you're tasting the end
   product, the fruit of someone's labor and attention to detail.*

3. **Creating in the office:**
   Observations are re-dubbed **Fuel***. The Fuel is correspondingly mapped
   over to actual UX processes / artifacts which I call* **Opportunity***:
   wireframing, user interviews, testing and refinement, etc.*

The reason I prefer large-paper format over whiteboard is that each point of the journey is tangibly represented in Lego form (Fig 4.1). For my workshop in Sweden, the Legos themselves became oft-photographed celebrities; to the participants, they provided an unexpected degree of visual interest and engagement with the space. They got people intrigued, talking, and added just the right amount of playfulness to lower their collective guard and sharing.

To get the ball rolling in Stockholm, I cited a personal example of something I had observed that very morning on my walk from the hotel to the event venue: two fathers pushing their child in a stroller, and a teddy bear that had been dropped onto the sidewalk. Another person—moving at a morning commute's pace in the opposite direction—halted her steps, picked up the bear, and caught back up with the family to reunite beloved stuffed animal and child. Human connection and compassion: the precise values our work demands.

This story sparked momentum within the group, and their own observations soon followed. This process—mapping observations-to-takeaways—benefits from such momentum, but can also take some coaching to cull. As we're training the eye and mind to observe and process experiences that would typically be dismissed over the course of a day, this coaching is vital and intrinsic to the workshop's long-lasting value.

As with observing, a similar evolution of perception is required when we get back to the office and shift into "design mode" at our desks. This is when our takeaways become fuel (both perceptually, and verbally on the sheet of paper); fuel that ignites opportunity against our design process and deliverables.

Using the initial examples I gave in this section of a stranger pausing to give directions, or in visiting a local café, a sample filled-in sheet can end up looking like the opposite page (Fig 4.2).

You'll notice the Takeaways from both the Commute and Pause columns net out with the following:

- Empathy
- Shape / form
- Process-to-quality
- Curation

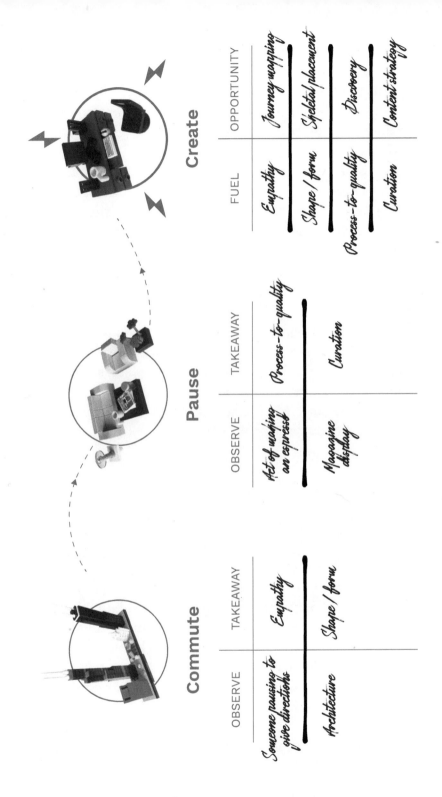

Commute

OBSERVE	TAKEAWAY
Someone pausing to give directions	Empathy
Architecture	Shape / form

Pause

OBSERVE	TAKEAWAY
Act of making an espresso	Process-to-quality
Magazine display	Curation

Create

FUEL	OPPORTUNITY
Empathy	Journey mapping
Shape / form	Skeletal placement
Process-to-quality	Discovery
Curation	Content strategy

Now, focus on the "Create" column specifically. As I noted a moment ago, those Takeaways are now dubbed Fuel, and that Fuel informs tangible and process-based Opportunity: How do their platform or device or connectivity impact their journey? How are they feeling? Are they lost? Are they delighted? Are they frustrated?

Or, what about "process-to-quality" through observing that barista at his craft? In UX, before producing any sort of tangible artifact, the vital process of Discovery helps researchers and designers genuinely understand people they're creating for, and the issues they're up against. They're taking the necessary time to listen, learn, research, and question. This process at the beginning of an initiative directly informs overall quality of a product at its completion.

As part of our professional livelihoods, we need to have the ability to share someone else's feelings or experiences by imagining what it would be like to be in that person's situation; that is, quite literally, the definition of "empathy" (thanks, Cambridge Dictionary). Having actual observed experiences in that regard provides us added human-centered fuel toward that imperative responsibility.

The Tools

As we've discussed, the goal of this workshop is to get people accustomed to observing, processing, and leveraging-as-fuel in their creative process: the tangible informing the digital informing the ultimate human experience. Ensuring this fuel is always at your fingertips brings the "leveraging" portion home and is the secret sauce to this exercise.

At Design Day, near the conclusion of the workshop I gave each attendee a Chicago flag-branded Field Notes memo book. Though they imparted a touch of (my) home while in Scandinavia, for your purposes the brand and Chicago-ness of the notepad are ultimately irrelevant; its scale and form factor are the point. Our target should be the size of an average smartphone.

In order to have an ever-present fountain of inspiration always on-hand (and in their back pocket), I want you to—as moments present themselves—**document** (mobile phone) and **record** (memo book). When you see a moment of empathy, or a magazine display that's curated, or the shape and form of architecture piercing the sky: take a picture with your smartphone, and jot down the corresponding context of the moment. If your memo book is at home, add a few words to a consistent text file on your phone instead.

So the next time you're sketching hierarchical placement of shape and form for a wireframe, or defining the top tasks of a journey map, or have a few minutes before your next conference call gets under way while participants ask each other *"Can you hear me?"* you'll have human-centered fuel at your fingertips.

Hackathons and Retreats

There are many companies out there who offer professional development-based perks to their employees: online courses, association memberships, and industry conference trips among them. For example, when I was with Nansen the conference trip option was already a part of their cultural offering; something I keenly considered as I weighed my options.

The one stipulation was that, upon an employee's conference return, they present back to the company what they got out of the opportunity and the (potential) worth to other team members in attending next year. Not a bad deal, right? It's a strong demonstration that employees are seen as much more than instruments of client project execution and showed that we wanted our team members to grow and evolve.

Inspiration acquired from conferences in our industry can be quite valuable: you're listening to thought leaders present on tech trends, their professional experience, and insights into where design and development are headed. Beyond an overall sense of being recharged and re-energized toward our crafts, the end goal is to infuse this new learning back into our daily work and active projects.

When you're in a seat at a conference, it's called **passive learning**. By and large, you're not so much engaging with the material and speaker as much as absorbing nuggets of wisdom. Focusing on a notepad to jot down a resonated thought or grabbing a mobile device to tweet a sound bite serves as a pervasive distraction against the overall experience. You're being talked at from afar, with the dynamism of conversational exchange lost.

Active Learning

We can do more toward the benefits obtained by sending someone to a conference, and at a fraction the cost. Let's consider the spirit of a **hackathon** instead.

At the highest level, a hackathon encourages a group of people to create (programmatically *and* visually, ideally) in unison and produce something amazing together, typically over the course of a few days or weekends. This partnered problem solving builds a shared creative energy that lasts well beyond the event's conclusion. It's why so many people love to participate.

It's this idea—of people coming together, creating something amazing without the constraints of the context of client work—that inspired Clearleft to start their Hack Farm concept.

Beginning in 2011, and repeated annually since, the entirety of their agency has come together as a single team to build something unique and fun. Having rented a farmhouse away from the buzz of the city for their inaugural event, and going into it without a plan of what to hack, they came away with Map Tales, a tool to help people tell stories illustrated with maps.

I tried to push Andy Budd a bit to ascertain how challenging it was for their company to shut down operations for a week, put projects and deliverables on hold, and trek into rural England to get away from it all. Despite my prodding, the fish weren't biting.

There was no challenge, no trepidation, he explained; it was the most natural thing in the world for them to do.

"We wanted to do it as a retreat or an escape from commercialization. We went in with the idea that whatever we built wasn't going to be a thing. We don't want to launch it and ship it and make millions. We want to have a bit of fun. We want to explore new ways of thinking, new ways of working."

And though Clearleft is a mid-size company, size isn't a limiting factor toward the same cultural support. Twitter's quarterly internal Hack Week has yielded everything from practical functionality like the ability to archive your own tweets to the more fanciful open-source photo-tweeting birdhouse. Many organizations have seen the value of these types of internal retreats; the wins, they are aplenty.

Leveraging Clearleft's Hack Farm as our model, my friend and colleague Andreas Carlsson and I started a program a few years back called Wintercamp. With the very goal of fostering active-over-passive learning, everyone in the business—all roles from our global locations—was invited to centralize at a retreat in rural Sweden to create something together. The process of what we'd build was a learning process: too pre-planned (going in with designated options) at first, and then not planned enough (going in and figuring it out on-site). And ultimately, as in Little Red Riding Hood's porridge, just right: a couple "tracks" (ideas, more broadly) over a few very fluid teams.

We developed tools we could use in our daily process once back on home turf. We'd participate in open collaboration and non-adversarial discussion. We put faces to names of people only previously known from an email chain. Our titles were irrelevant; the teams we formed, flat and collegial.

When participants weren't focused on work, they'd cook for one another, have endless discussions about their mutual craft(s), and enjoy the surrounding expansive grounds and leisure activities. At the end of each day, the various project teams would present to each other what they've accomplished, what the pitfalls were, and solicit open and honest feedback.

People returned to their home offices recharged. Invigorated and inspired by their global coworkers, they acted as living embodiments of the culture. The projects worked on at Wintercamp continued as formal entities once we were back at our desks, which kept the momentum going. And teams functioned more effectively, having worked toward common goals and made deeper personal connections.

All Work and No Play Makes Jack a Dull Boy

The rural environment in which Wintercamp is held is a deliberate selection, conducive to outdoor enjoyment and activities that promote humanizing the experience. That said, the start-up atmosphere of Wintercamp had often compromised our participants actually *getting outdoors*. People had become so charged from creating that they've rarely left the cabin.

And so, Carlsson and I reevaluated the experience and turned it into something else. Enter [x]Camp.

[x]Camp was conceived specifically to get people interacting with their environment and thinking away from their laptops. To have them rethink problems and solutions by utilizing their surroundings, and to have those surroundings supply maximum, unending inspiration.

I secured the Hauer Ranch in Moab, Utah, just minutes from Arches National Park (Fig 4), to provide exactly such an experience. With a dozen co-workers distributed between three SUV's, we hashed out some rough themes to work on over the four-hour drive from Salt Lake City down to Moab. Inclusive of the benefit of its surroundings and isolation, the Ranch was also selected because its Wi-Fi connection was, as advertised, passable at best. Basic browsing and email checking were about as involved in the digital world as we could get. And that was the point.

Day One consisted of a five-hour guided hike in the national park's aptly named Fiery Furnace (Fig 4.1) to reset our thinking, set the tone for the camp, and let the environment refuel us. Over the

Fig 4: Arches National Park, Moab, Utah.

following three days developers sketched database diagrams in the crimson Utah dirt, stand-ups were held upon ancient stone cliffs, and passionate dialogues evolved over wee-hour campfires.

This is a company culture extending its boundaries beyond its walls. It's a tangible demonstration of support and respect that an elevator pitch could never deliver.

Via thoughtful planning, lots of research, and trial-and-error, Carlsson and I developed two ongoing internal camps that have became a staple to the company's identity. People I'd interviewed for roles on my team while at that company had directly cited the camps as the reason they reached out. This positive outward and inward buzz is invaluable, but when it comes down to brass tacks, at what cost does this all come to the company which ultimately foots the bill?

Well, if a business uses the thought of "costliness" as a demerit against the act of sending employees to conferences, I can tell you this about our camps: they come in at about a third the cost, per person, in a comparative sense. By doing advanced logistical

FIG 4.1: THE FIERY FURNACE, ARCHES NATIONAL PARK, MOAB, UTAH.

planning, centralizing a location to stay, and cooking for one another on a daily basis, costs are mitigated drastically. We've held our versions abroad and within the States, but the duration, scale, and activities can always be adjusted to suit a designated budget.

Process Pairing is Priceless

There's value in the smart planning of an offsite trip: both for quality of team interactions at the ultimate destination and the business' bottom line.

At the highest level, however, there is one cost we simply *cannot* afford to incur: a disconnection between culture and creation. Offsite camps, presentation mentorship, fika breaks, and first-day Fridays have a human-centered core that begs for a counterpart in our design process. Let's look at why.

CHAPTER

5

Humans
at the
Heart of
It All

/ 6

Putting people first—at the workplace and in our design process—
yields an intuitive, successful end product and an endless fountain
of inspiration.

Over the previous four chapters, our dialogue has been
largely framed through the lens of human-centered culture
and interactions: empathy, respect, and compassion. But what
specifically of the manner in which we actually create within said
culture? We need to design for people (and with people) using the
same core principles with which we treat one another within a
creative culture. **Human-centered design is the answer.**

As it shall be with culture, so shall it be with design. It's an
ultimately simple notion, and simplicity will be our entry point to
expanding this concept (in comicbook form, no less).

IN 1996,
IT WAS A
SIMPLER TIME
IN TECHNOLOGY.

IBM's Deep Blue defeated chess grandmaster Gary Kasparov for the first time.

Walking into an electronic store yielded no trace whatsoever of any Apple product or peripheral, making decision a non-descision.

Desktop icons on a Mac (8-bit, 256-color) were hand-crafted pixel-by-pixel in a 32×32 grid, via resource editing app ResEdit.

CONVERSELY,
IN MANY WAYS,
THINGS WERE ALSO
FAR MORE COMPLEX...

Approachable is Preferable

There's a phrase for the ease in which we're able to think about things: "cognitive fluency." In user experience design the impacts on fluency are expansive: how easy is a font to read? How strong is the accessible contrast ratio? How intuitive is a workflow? How clear is the copy in guiding you along? The simpler things are to process, the easier they are to engage with.

As we saw in the mini graphic novel a couple pages back, customizing your Mac's interface with pixel-based icons during the mid-90s was common; doing so spoke as much to personalization as it did to thumbing your nose at the beige PC towers that defined the norm. While control panels such as Kaleidoscope quickly skinned your entire UI with a single click, I and other icon designers of the time ("iconists") dove into desktop iconography, crafting pixel-based mini-mosaics under ridiculous constraints: 256 colors on a 32×32 grid, made in the resource editing app ResEdit.

ResEdit itself was rudimentary yet incredibly robust (Fig 5). Last officially released by Apple in 1994, it was primarily a tool for developers to create and edit resources in the resource fork architecture Macs used to rely on. One such resource, "ICON," was the focus and, pixel by pixel, we employed common practices as the means to disparate stylistic ends:

- Manually dithering via finite tonal variations to simulate depth
- Stacking pixel units of a shape's outline conservatively, to avoid "jaggies" and smooth edges
- Faux anti-aliasing of harsh edges via the six available non-alpha-transparent grey swatches

From system-level icons to household objects to movie characters to original creations, a community of creators crafted downloadable icons that graced the desktops of millions of people the world over. The cognitive read of these icons had to connect, engage, and convey their identifiable meaning instantly amongst the clutter of folders and files.

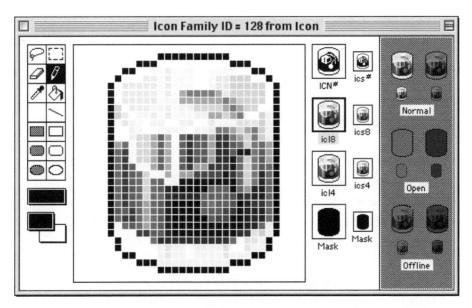

FIG 5: THE RESEDIT INTERFACE BEING USED TO CREATE AN "OLD FASHIONED" ICON OF MY DESIGN.

Good Design is as Little Design as Possible

Utter the name Dieter Rams around any designer and immediate visceral thoughts about his work come to mind: simplicity. Intuitiveness. Aesthetic. Thoughtfulness.

Rams, a German industrial designer who was largely responsible for the design of Braun's consumer products over his 40 years with the company, is considered one of the most influential product designers of the 20th century. *"Good design is as little design as possible"* is the last of his "10 principles of good design," also fondly referred to as the "10 Commandments of Design." The full text of the tenth principle notes that good design:

> *"...is as little design as possible: Less, but better – because it concentrates on the essential aspects, and the products are not burdened with non-essentials. Back to purity, back to simplicity."*

"...concentrates on the essential aspects..."
"...not burdened with non-essentials."

These points should immediately resonate with user experience designers. In the Mobile First methodology we understand that, because of the confines of smaller viewports, we need to be hyperaware of interface clutter as we design. Clear priority must be given to the core actions a person needs to take; we must stay cognizant of content download speeds, the time to complete the most vital tasks in a given workflow, and all the cognitive dissonance of the world around them. Away from the banner ads and multiple calls to action of an unruly desktop-sized presentation, we (visually) communicate and present with a laser focus: *"Back to purity, back to simplicity."*

This is all to say: people gravitate toward ideas that are simple to understand (cognitive fluency). Notably, it's not merely simplicity for simplicity's sake *("Less, but better")*: communicating simply is to be compassionate to the human beings we're communicating *with.* Is someone engaging with our experience while holding a smartphone with one hand on the subway? Are they interacting with a vital workflow in the midst of a crisis? Or managing account information on an archaic terminal on a noisy factory floor? The possibilities are infinite. Restating a point from the first paragraph of the book: "Mobile First? In reality, it's *humans* first."

You Are What You Eat

We cannot preach outwardly about empathy for those we're designing for (**human beings**) if, as designers, researchers, architects, developers, we're not supporting each other. *"You are what you eat,"* Jeffrey Zeldman quipped when I bounced this point off him.

To get ourselves in the groove of identifying the points of synergy between human-centered design and culture, now let's consider some ways simplicity impacts the latter.

In Chapter 3 we talked about how billable hours—while

unquestionably vital to a business keeping its lights on—are not the sole means by which to judge an employee's value. That said, time entry is likely something a large part of us have had to endure along the way in our careers. I carefully selected the word "endure" because, if you're like me, time entry typically gets left as the last thing on your list for the day. Or, the week... or *cough* month. Why? Because often, time entry is a shitty process. Tedium. Clunky interfaces.

Many tools selected at the upper echelons of business get implemented without a collaborative dialogue with the very people who will use them. And often, these tools remain in place for eons due to initial expense and, as time drags on, an overall lack of priority. And if you think your people can't sense the indifference, you're fooling yourself

What's the most likely way to get people to enter their time daily? How about the most effective method to get expenses submitted? Corporate intranets are notorious for languishing for years as unintuitive, cobbled-together monstrosities that only the longest-tenured of employees can successfully navigate. Accessing documents and vital or timely information can be an exercise in futility. Beyond the mundane tasks many of us loathe, tool complexity adds another barrier to entry that makes a lack of engagement a near guarantee.

Cognitive fluency in business-dependent tool design increases the likelihood of their adoption, and there are copious intuitive, effectively designed options on the market today. The value of simplicity in this type of tooling, then, is clear: essential business processes are executed with consistency and timeliness. Employee engagement is enriched when tools are implemented with them in mind, and, above all, a culture of people-first support is exemplified in practice.

Simplicity also means "clarity." I used the GDS example earlier regarding their list of things that "it's OK to do" posted on walls throughout their office. New employees can immediately ascertain what benefits the culture affords without confusion—or at the very least, they won't hesitate to ask. And zooming out to a more macro level, overall clarity in communication within a business is equally paramount. Scott M. Cutlip's book *Effective Public Relations* introduced the concept of the "7 C's of Communication," which have largely been adapted to business communication, too. "Clarity" is core to the list:

> *"The message must be put in simple terms. Words used must have exactly the same meaning to the sender as they do to the receiver. Complex messages must be distilled into simpler terms, and the farther a message must travel, the simpler it should be."*

Removing barriers—in recognition, interaction, and communication—is key to achieving simplicity, and facilitating a connection.

A Connection is What it's All About

A "human-centered mindset" means people are at the center of everything in a business: empathy and compassion guide our hand across personnel, process, and product.

Zeroing in on process, human-centered design (HCD) was largely popularized by the design firm IDEO, who were early pioneers in this way of creating. They've designed everything from the first Apple Mouse, to a high-tech kidney delivery system, to Levi's digitally connected Commuter Trucker Jacket, to an intuitive and accessible voting experience for residents of Los Angeles. IDEO also teaches online courses on their people-first approach, runs in-person workshops, and published their methods via *The Field Guide to Human-Centered Design*. In short: they know their shit. I was fortunate to tour their Chicago office a handful of years ago and observe a bit of their environment first-hand.

The value of HCD is that a design team's subjectivity is completely removed from the equation: by being inclusive of the very human beings we're creating for, every step of the way, the end product is an objective, intuitive experience.

IDEO is driven by empathy, which they say fuels *"a deep*

A "HUMAN-CENTERED
MINDSET" MEANS PEOPLE ARE
AT THE CENTER OF EVERYTHING
IN A BUSINESS: EMPATHY AND
COMPASSION GUIDE OUR HAND
ACROSS PERSONNEL, PROCESS,
AND PRODUCT.

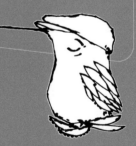

understanding of the problems and realities of the people you are designing for." Six core steps define their process:

1. **Observation**
   Understanding the people they're designing for
2. **Ideation**
   Brainstorming ideas culled from observation
3. **Rapid prototyping**
   Building simple prototypes made out of effectively anything that conveys an idea
4. **User feedback**
   Gathering input by getting the simple prototypes into the hands of actual people
5. **Iteration**
   Refining based on the above; cyclical between 4 and 5 until an intuitive, usable solution emerges
6. **Implementation**
   Releasing into the world (and cyclically going back to step 1)

HCD-driven firms outside of IDEO will have variations on these facets (from a step's moniker in an apples-to-apples sense to more steps overall, etc.), but the overarching principles and end goals are the same: advocate for people, include them throughout the design process, and refine based on real-world usage.

Human-Centered Design is Personal

Currently, I'm the Vice President of Human-Centered Design and Development at bswift, a SaaS benefits enrollment and administration firm owned by a Fortune 10 parent company. Founded in 1996, bswift's goal is to use technology to simplify the administration of healthcare, reduce costs, and connect consumers to the resources they need.

As an industry, healthcare in the U.S. is a convoluted, complex system of plans, policies, and networks. People struggle to navigate these hurdles for themselves and those they care for (or depend on), often under dire circumstances. At this point in my evolution as a designer—much more than the work I was doing in the agency world—*healthcare* is where I felt I and the application of human-centered design could genuinely do good for people.

When I joined bswift to lead their UX Team, they had a strong core group of designers and front-end developers operating as a shared service across multiple products. Taking time to observe and understand the manner in which the team was engaging with the organization (and vice versa), I put together two plans:

1. Augmenting a healthy baseline culture (at the business level) to further support, inspire, and cultivate talents at the team level
2. Evolving a UX team into an HCD practice

When a person (or people) starts a business, they typically put together a business plan articulating future goals and the means by which to achieve them. When I'm building out a team or taking a lead on the culture at the organizational level, I put together a **culture plan**. You cannot expect success to happen magically when starting a business and, similarly, a culture's pillars, planning, and goals need an equal level of thoughtful curation and respect.

That said, point 1 above encapsulated much of what you've read to this point: pausing with intent. Educating on delivering effective, objective, and actionable feedback. Refueling via Creative Inspiration Wednesdays. Implementing The New Day One for new team members. Championing a positive environment of support, humility, and respect. Transitioning a practice that existed before your arrival within a large organization, however—and how the organization itself engages with said practice—is not a trivial feat, nor does it happen overnight.

It all begins with education, and my work at bswift would be no exception.

As a human-centered design practice would ultimately impact our project timelines, team expenses, my future hiring needs, how we sell and articulate our products and process, etc., I began the "HCD Roadshow" to connect with stakeholders within our organization. These dialogues largely revolved around HCD's value: to people, to our products, to innovation, and to our market differentiation. It was imperative to be as transparent as possible in articulating this process-based evolution so both my team and the business were on the same page and set up for success.

Evolving, upsizing, maintaining, or supporting anything at scale (culture and design practice, in this instance) within a larger organization is predicated upon results and their value to the business. For example, a healthy culture means employee retention, brand equity, etc. Human-centered design means quality, adoption of product, innovation, etc. These things are measurable.

Just as data should inform our design (over driving decision), metrics inform the conversation of "value to the organization" when advocating for evolution. In previous roles as well as this one, I've utilized this approach when building and growing a design practice as well as elevating healthy culture from the team level to the organization level. In both instances, the human connection leads. And in both instances, cost and resources are needed from the business to facilitate the change.

Approaching stakeholders responsible for the (financial and procedural) support of growth, with human-centric value and applicable metrics in-hand, combines people-first responsibility with business ROI.

Continuing the process of building an HCD practice at bswift, I worked with product owners and teams broadly to establish how we could best engage with them, and them with us. The project intake process needed to evolve from the UX team receiving a stack of executables to having an actionable seat at the table from inception through completion. With the team at the table, the very people we're advocating for also pulled up a chair.

Timelines (and expectations) had to be adjusted to account for the vital Observation process. Before pencil met paper, dialogues with our clients and their employees had to become the norm: there needed to be time for discovery. Time for listening. Time for research. Time for potential workshops. Time for synthesis and reporting. "UX" needed to find its home as part of our process and tangible artifacts, not as the identity of the team. By previously educating the organization on HCD's value and bringing them along for the ride, we nullified any potential procedural concerns.

Looking inward, the process adjustments I was proposing required us to formalize and grow a research discipline. I ensured applicable key roles were added into the hiring plan, and then shifted my focus outside the company walls. Understanding that the confines of our office were a limiter to the team connecting with people, I trained them on how to conduct ethnographic research. By observing on client premises, we began to gain a physical and spatial understanding of human-to-human and human-to-experience interactions that a video conference call could never yield. We also needed to recognize our own personal biases via an inclusive process, so the HCD team developed a recruiting initiative to fuel in-house usability testing. To support this, I worked with our Operations manager to secure a meeting room as a newly dedicated usability lab for our group, building out and tangibly cementing a home base.

Culled from a human-centered process, we created new artifacts to complement the team's work and ultimately fuel connection, and fashioned personas from copious dialogues with those who engage with our products. We derived commonalities across varied demographics, inclusive of age, the platform they used to enroll in their benefits, level of tech savvy, prescription needs, and dependents, amongst others. These personas helped give a soul to our UX design, particularly when coupled with journey and empathy maps across systemic workflows (from logging in to receiving their confirmation statement, for example). Potential pain points and areas of confusion (or clarity, or delight) were identified, iterated upon, and shepherded into the usability testing process for further iteration.

Across design, research, and front-end development, I continued to staff a diverse team to bring divergent points of view and different skill sets to our process to reflect the reality of the world we're creating for. Our non-homogenous culture would also be directly better for it.

CREATING **WITH** COMPASSION IN AN ENVIRONMENT FUELED **BY** COMPASSION MEANS WE NEVER LOSE SIGHT OF WHAT IT'S ALL ABOUT: PEOPLE.

Connecting the Dots

Two plans: one for design, one for culture.

What I've found is that the DNA between both dynamics must be inextricable from one another. Creating *with* compassion in an environment fueled *by* compassion means we never lose sight of what it's all about: people. Beyond functioning in this manner because "it's the right thing to do," quality of work, loyalty internally (team) and externally (users), and product innovation are all benefits to reap.

Earlier we talked through the concept of "simplicity" and its application to creation and environment. Now, let's revisit a few other examples of healthy benchmarks from a creative culture as we've discussed in this book:

- Slowing down / pausing with intent
- Everyone has a seat at the table
- The New Day One

In taking a focused look at these facets, their correlation to HCD is readily apparent:

Culture: Slowing down / pausing with intent
Design: Discovery / observation

The Swedish concept of *fika* transcends a mere "coffee break." It's about slowing down, the act of pausing during a typical day and making time to have a dialogue with someone (though a good cup of coffee is a vital part). I ensure this time is not only a known quantity within my team's creative culture, but that it's protected and actively utilized.

Instead of getting a product manager's Powerpoint wireframe in your inbox with a request to "make it look nice" or a client's request to crank out a design for their approval by EOD, we *must* slow down to understand the people who will be interacting with our design (and the design's potential impact on others, the environment and community in which it will be used, and so on). Rushing to get something done to tick an account manager's client-appeasement box at the expense of the human experience is to sacrifice empathy, quality, and any prospect of innovation.

Culture: Everyone has a seat at the table
Design: Inclusion

As the very definition of cultural transparency, Nick Sarillo's pizza parlors tack their full financial statements to a wall, daily, for all employees to see. Everyone's hourly wage is listed on a nearby whiteboard, with the means to make more money articulated in tandem (training in more areas of business = increased hourly wage). Many managers have worked their way up in this manner, and offer training to other employees who wish to advance by taking on more responsibility. This is about collaboration yielding success to both the employee and the business, the sharing of information, and access for all; key dynamics of an inclusive culture.

Inclusion in the design process enables us, as creators, to recognize our own personal biases. By identifying the exclusion in our work, we humbly set aside our assumptions; connecting with people from diverse communities, building empathy, will expand our product's reach (access). Via engaging humans throughout our design process, listening to them, and usability testing iteratively, objective solutions that yield innovation follow suit.

Culture: The New Day One
Design: Ethnography

The New Day One concept evolves an employee's first day from formulaic and sterile into directly personal and custom. Via the "Inspiration" portion of the day and venturing away from the office, we gain insight into a new team member as an individual that transcends what folio work can yield. What physical aspects of their selected location have impacted who they are? How did it inspire their way of creating, or approaching problems?

Understanding the impact of spatial dynamics on an individual is vital toward an individualistic, yet ultimately holistic, view.

Ethnographic research provides an environmental context to human interaction that a video-conference interview could never yield. Through direct observation, ethnography is the qualitative study of human beings in their native environment. Is the individual sitting in a high-traffic area in an office, causing frequent distraction from their work? Are they a field worker primarily utilizing a mobile device in direct sunlight, yielding paramount color contrast needs? By making research truly *human*, we gain an understanding of how those we observe see the world and how they ultimately engage with it.

For the Greater Good

Greater Good Studio (GGS) is a social impact-focused human-centered design firm co-founded by Sara Cantor Aye and George Aye. Their business is located within the Logan Share, a co-working space they also founded in Chicago's Logan Square neighborhood.

I reached out to the Studio to ask if I could stop by their space and observe a "morning in the life" view of their process: culture and design, organically, as both unfolded. Without hesitation, Sara (a former Northwestern University instructor) extended me an offer to join the team for observation. After signing a non-disclosure agreement, we agreed on a date for my visit.

When I arrived on a Monday morning, George (formerly of IDEO) greeted me with a cup of coffee and walked me up the stairs into the naturally well-lit Logan Share space. I noticed the open seating in the co-working section was already nearly full, as he gave me a tour of the "configuration by human need and intent"-based layout and active-project areas. On long single sheets of cardboard suspended by custom-built fasteners, entire lifecycles of project-centric human-centered design artifacts were on display. Once a project is deployed, George explained, the cardboard is detached and saved for forthcoming iteration, with fresh sheets re-fastened to form the partitions of a new project space thereafter.

The six core steps of the Studio's HCD process manifest themselves in the following way:

1. **Framing**
   Defining questions to answer and people to engage
2. **Research**
   Learning from people about their needs and values
3. **Synthesis**
   Finding patterns of behavior and areas of opportunity
4. **Concepting**
   Creating a high volume of new ideas
5. **Prototyping**
   Making tangible mock-ups and gathering feedback
6. **Piloting**
   Testing solutions in real time with real people

As a team, GGS functions via a working method called ROWE (Results Only Work Environment), a concept leveraged from Cali Ressler and Jody Thompson's book *Why Work Sucks and How to Fix It: The Results-Only Revolution*. Taken from an article on the Studio's blog, they describe the practice within GGS like this:

> *"The basic principle behind ROWE is that staff doesn't need to be supervised, when given the tools, clear expectations, and deadlines people will not only do their work, but do it better than if they were trying to fit into a mold. Within GGS, this practice is exercised by very diligent calendar management, clear deadlines, expectations on deliverables, and Cookie Rewards (little treats we give each other if we have to move something on the calendar)."*

Once a month the entire team pauses for a five-hour, non-client project block of time called "internal day." This time is reserved for studio-centric things: team members sharing learnings from conferences they've attended, how to improve internal practices, past project debriefs, etc. It's the act of pausing with intent, in full effect.

Sara arrived a few minutes into my tour of the space, and the GGS team's "BD charrette" was the first employee gathering (remote and in-person) of the morning. "BD" stands for "business development," and in a cozy seating area, everyone had a seat at the table in all senses of the phrase. Sara and George ran through the status of a current request for proposal, then each team member had the opportunity to voice their opinion about whether the RFP should be pursued based on how it aligned with GGS's (and their employees') personal, values. Everyone was heard; every voice was respected.

The dialogue eventually shifted to another potential new client, this time with GGS at the presentation stage. Again, everyone at the table gave their feedback on Sara and George's presentation plan of attack and, again, every team member's voice carried equal value and weight. The studio-wide inclusion in the business owners' decision making was genuine, effortless, and natural.

Forty-five minutes later, the group made a physical transition to a few nearby couches; less than a three-foot walk, as I eyed it. I inquired about the very minor spatial change for this next leg of the meeting and was told, "There's a difference in purpose, so we transition to a different space." Each member of the team then took their turn describing their weekend in three words:

"Sunshine, beach, baking."

I got my turn as well. Changing the energy on those couches, from new business to being focused on the individual, made for a palpable climate change. In a few words everyone had a sense of what their teammates got up to over the weekend, eliciting smiles and planting the seeds for future dialogues throughout the pauses-with-intent over the rest of the day.

Next: "validations." In this final portion of the meeting (pre-project status), anyone who wanted to articulate their appreciation for a team member over the previous week did so. One person recognized their co-worker for their selfless collaboration, taking time from their own project work to help theirs get client-ready on time. Similar-but-unique "thanks" emerged from varied people;

no one was required to speak up, but everyone did.

After project updates I sat with Sara for a one-on-one to chat over coffee. I asked her about the synergies between their HCD process and how she interacts with her team in the office:

"I think where it's actually become more intentional and obvious has been with our staff who are not trained designers. Operations folks, or our community manager, etc. I've had to say, 'I want you to be a designer about this' (whatever 'this' is). 'We are your users, you're trying to get us to do our timesheets, or clean up the kitchen, etc. Observe. Talk to people. Figure out our motivations. Summarize everything you've learned, and then have ideas.'

As a designer, I am constantly designing at every level. I'm designing deliverables in many cases for clients, or coaching our teams to design deliverables. I'm also designing process by which we work by writing proposals, scoping, etc. And at the highest level, I'm designing our company. I'm designing our culture based on our customs and traditions and policies (the hard and the soft) every day. My users are not hypothetical, they're actual people."

When All is Not Good

Sara went on to cite how her previous work experience shaped the leader she is today:

"I think a lot of my design choices are based in (unhealthy dynamics) with prior employers. Where decisions were not made transparently, everything financial was completely opaque. Lots of lack of trust with other employees. It's been so critical that I've had bad experiences so I can now clearly say: let's not do that."

The tactics, mindsets, organizational shifts, and operational flexibility discussed in this book are predicated upon a simple truth: a company presently supports and operates as a creative culture, or it's genuinely willing to evolve to become one. Along the way, I've been primarily speaking to those who are in a position to help implement change; even at a small scale. But what about when you're not in a position to be heard, or the position to help facilitate change?

Reality isn't always unicorns and rainbows. Bad experiences can impact us all. For example, the fabric of a company's creative culture can become irreparably frayed thanks to management changes, acquisition, or it can lack sustainability. Whether these circumstances reveal themselves over years or overnight, your passion and evolution should never be their casualty.

Sometimes, creating within an environment that's the best fit for your growth and passions means finding a new opportunity.

6

Your
Cultural
Match

/ 6

Ending an unhealthy relationship is a painful endeavor.

It's an experience many of us have likely had at some point. In a divorce, there's a division of assets and the loss of years of investment. In a break-up, there's the acknowledgment that the honeymoon period wasn't indicative of a long-term, sustainable fit. The experience is rife with disappointment and letdown when reality hasn't met expectations. The same can be said for the moment you look around your workplace and realize: "I've got to get out of here."

Finding your cultural best fit isn't a swipe-left or swipe-right matchmaking process. It requires research, patience, and honesty about your goals, desires, and work habits. As a passionate, dedicated, hungry individual looking to grow and thrive, you deserve nothing less than your perfect cultural match.

There's no "easy way" covered in this chapter. As with everything else we've covered, the mindset of putting humans first—in this case, you—will serve as our compass while navigating new career options.

We began this book with a healthy, human-centered, engaging Day One. Now, we'll conclude by revisiting it, albeit under different circumstances: those that begin to sound your internal alarm.

One Small Step for Gain

As with the Apple onboarding example cited in Chapter 1, there are hallmarks of a first day in any role that can be considered "standard welcoming gestures": intro handshakes and name exchanges. Going out for lunch with your new peers (and not footing the bill). New hardware and some swag. Broadly, these are nice nods toward a potentially solid culture.

Conversely, as I noted earlier through some of my personal experiences on first days, there can be some fairly immediate overt signs of deeper, culturally problematic issues. Getting lobbed into a project within minutes of being on premises. Having no one, save for the person who hired you, aware of your arrival. Cots near the cubicle farm (and people still in them).

As such, we need to take a look at how to react in the instance the culture appears to be not what it seemed initially. Why didn't the company's actual methods (symptoms) come up during the interview process? Did they hide the cots last week? You'd done your homework on the company, had some good dialogue leading up to this point; where did things go astray?

As stressful as first days can unfortunately be, you need to distinguish between the Day One jitters and your gut's revulsion against legitimate red flags. When targeting potential new opportunities, did you seek out this company because of their external brand? Or was it due to what you knew of their internal culture? Dynamic brands and dynamic creative cultures do not always go hand in hand.

Let me tell you about the Day Five Principle, or "Why Every Recruiter in the Galaxy Will Loathe Me Momentarily (#WERGWLMM)."

Let's say your first day has yielded some warning signs that are keenly opposed to your ability to do your best work. Without being overly reactionary, and presuming the best of your new employer, sometimes there are days when things just don't sync up. Like any individual human being, offices or teams can also have bad days where things are out of whack with the overall creative energy and in responding to client needs. For this, let's take some calming breaths, fall into our Jedi peace, and give the company the benefit of the doubt for a standard business week: through Day Five.

Over the course of these five days, and beyond the already noted obvious signs of an unhealthy culture, watch how your teammates interact with one another and with your team leader. Is there a dialogue, or a monologue? Observe what people are doing to collaborate, energize, and inspire one another. If you're ascertaining a grim outlook on those things, or if time given to due process in design and development is relegated to being reactionary to line items on a project brief, the company's creative culture may not be the best fit.

Much of the above can be directly inquired about during your initial conversations and the interview process to mitigate any surprises come Day One and ensure the best cultural fit. We'll look at this process shortly.

There's a grand work up to having taken a new role. That is to say, you've told your friends, your family, maybe taken to social media to let followers know, etc. From this Day One-onward, there's now a steady paycheck en route. Likely some health insurance. Perhaps some sort of 401k. All of these things considered, there is no greater barometer in existence for the reality of your situation and the culture of the new organization than your gut. I don't take it lightly in the least when I say this: it's far better to sever ties quickly than to languish in a situation you absolutely know is wrong for you. Put more directly: get the hell out of there.

I realize what I'm advocating could earn me a few guffaws: "well, you can't do that!" And to that, my response is, well why not? At this point, you have built up momentum in marketing yourself to potential employers. You have your job listing web sites and industry contacts very recently "in play" on your behalf. The ultimate decision comes down to this: having an hour of potential awkwardness in a conversation with HR or a manager, or staying with a company for weeks, months, or years because you feel indebted or socially required. The gesture is also a wake-up call to the organization; your candor, an ice bucket boon to their culture and potentially the other disillusioned employees.

Anything that has culturally revealed itself so clearly in the first five days is a gift to you, your craft, your dignity, and your passion. In unhealthy cultures, sometimes these signs can take time to evolve. Before negativity becomes the norm, and the norm becomes a comfort, the freshness of what's transpiring is, in fact, your ally. It makes it easier to see, to assess, and to challenge what you're willing to accept.

Thinking Outside the Job Board

When you've found a creative culture that reveals itself as a lightning rod for your programmatic or design passion, you'll experience butterflies. Goosebumps. It needn't take having been burned previously in other roles, or on other Day One's, to know deep down that you've found something special. Your gut will plainly tell you this, too.

Your cultural match is out there. Unless you've got an "in" via your network and have a streamlined research and hiring experience, however, it's going to take effort to find it. Just as a creative culture applies human-centered ways of thinking that redefine "standard" business processes, I ask that you shift your way of thinking toward a human-centered, "non-standard" job search.

I'm not going to tell you how to use a job board or list out ways to start a dialogue with a recruiter. While of course incredibly valuable in your process, those are the lowest hanging of fruits on the career hunt tree.

Identify some companies you would love to work with and begin to investigate their story and the way they tell it. How do you feel they portray themselves? What seems most important to them? How do they speak about their people and their work? Which of those (people, or work) have preferential hierarchy in the navigation on their website?

Whether visually or in content, the quality of a company's body of work (product or service-based) is an obvious, readily ascertainable thing. The story behind the work is where their culture comes to light. At what cost was the work created? Was it collaboratively produced? Were the project constraints realistic? Was it via all-nighters for days or weeks on end at the expense of time for recharging or seeing their families?

Many job boards offer Yelp-style reviews of businesses from their past and current employees, providing a sampling of some "behind the curtains" cultural revelations. While helpful, there's a narrative behind the narrative there, and you're only ever going to get part of it with online research.

To truly grasp what the culture of a company you have an interest in is like, let's put it to the test right from the start: via human contact.

Reaching Out

In this role-seeking process, I'm encouraging you to try new avenues of contact and investigation. Passively lobbing a resume and cover letter over the digital fence does not do your passions, your voice, or your rightful place in a creative culture any semblance of justice.

Reach out to the business. Talk to them.

Companies largely have a "Contact" link in their global navigation, yes? Let's put that content to work. Find an appropriate person: General contact? Hiring manager? The person you suspect might work within the discipline in which you're interested? Reaching out over the phone affords ever-vital human interaction and is preferred; email provides the recipient time to respond if they're busy. If the job posting had a "No phone calls, please" qualifier, respect that; it's not a reveal against anything cultural. The responsible party for hiring simply may not be able to take copious calls throughout the course of their day.

"But what if they don't respond? What if they hang up, or shut the door in my face, or it compromises my chances?" you might ask.

Should any of the above occur, what you gain is an immediate insight into their culture, and how it treats other human beings (and potential colleagues). Jaan Orvet told me about an applicant who was looking into a company he recently worked with:

> "At the place I was recently with, we talked to a designer who really cares about culture. She was more than welcome to talk to people who have left (the company), and people who are presently employed there. And our clients. It can't be any other way."

If you have the opportunity after establishing a dialogue with an organization you've reached out to, talk to people who have left the company, at varying levels of hierarchy. If a culture is transparent and the business treats its people with respect, there's nothing to sweep under the rug. They'll appreciate that you care that much and won't hesitate to put you in contact with people that have left.

Knock Knock

The value of reaching out to a company of interest through phone or email is that, no matter the response, you'll learn something valuable about their culture.

Sometimes, there is no contact information available. Sometimes, you have no one "on the inside" vetting a business' culture or expediting your resume's routing process. To the human connection, and in ascertaining "a day in the life" of a business candidly, this can be an opportunity rather than roadblock:

How about knocking on their door?

"There was one place in particular where I didn't even remotely know anyone who had something to do with the company. I just went and rang the doorbell, and they opened. I thought I'd see: do they open the door? Who opens the door? And they thought I was really weird, so they let me in."

Orvet was intrigued about a UK business' culture, as he was considering them as an option for a new role. Outwardly, the company had an image of being somewhat cold, despite the tremendous work they produced; he sought to understand the face behind the curtain.

"Just from (ringing the doorbell), they understood something about me, and I thought it was kind of cool when I found out it was one of their senior project managers who opened the door. Everyone there took care of things around the office, opening the door, answering the phone, washing the dishes. They talked to me about why they had the image of being inaccessible. I learned so much."

Ultimately, through a thoughtful 20-minute conversation the employee had with him, it was clear to both sides that there wouldn't have been a cultural match. The fairytale ending to the story would have been that the company opened the door, there was an instant synergistic cultural love affair, and a job offer was extended at minute 21. That's not realistic, nor is it the point of knocking in the first place.

The gesture of a business opening the door and chatting with you is an excellent demonstration of a human-centered belief system. If they slam the door in your face (metaphorically...), you know you don't want to work there. Of course, the company might not be able to talk much at that point but get a sense for what they're doing. Listen to what they're saying. Do they think it's great that you turn up and you're showing initiative? Or, do they say "Oh no, you're the 12th person today to show up. I'm sorry, this doesn't work here."

Well, great: you've learned something about the business and their culture that a job posting cannot provide. Simply by knocking on the door.

The Usability of Résumé Design

When we think resume design, "usability" typically isn't one of the first things to spring to mind. An art director seeking a new position might create an 8-point typographic masterpiece that, while beautiful as a design, is not the best read of information. A developer may hammer out an exhaustive, experience-documenting, 4-page all-serif Word doc. While the ultimate opportunity you're targeting should organically shape the design and information contained in your résumé, clarity, quick-scannability, and definitive information hierarchy are absolutely vital.

As someone who's been in receipt of copious amounts of résumés in my various positions, the above examples are quite often not that far off reality. "Theme-designed" résumés (by that I mean designs in which the résumé layout in and of itself is intended as a showcase of your creative brand), while often visually and typographically stunning, can suffer from having key information not readily apparent on a visual scan basis. This can be a trade-off, but whichever approach you feel suits you best, there are some tactics you can employ in any scenario to ensure your information provides an easier read.

The Art of Scannability

A usability best practice, as it applies to digital design, is reserving a color for clickable items (buttons, text links, etc.) so it's immediately visually apparent I can take action upon them. We can leverage that broad concept, color usage as a visual cue, in a résumé.

Important to note: leveraging color enhances this experience. The design nor read of information are ultimately dependent upon its usage. We need to be keenly aware of those who are color blind in any design.

Consider the résumé of Jet Greyhound (Fig 6). He's using blue and orange as visually scannable, categorical devices (by "scannable" I mean the ability of our eyes to "grab on" to focused elements as they view content in layout). Viewing this example, blue directly pertains to Jet and the roles he's held, so we scan:

- Jet Greyhound
- Role Four
- Role Three
- Role Two
- Role One
- Degree, focus of study

Orange is used to denote locations and general subheads, and we scan:

- experience
  - Company Four
  - Company Three
  - Company Two
  - Company One
- education
  - University of Awesome
- skills

Jet Greyhound

contact@jetgreyhound.com
www.jetgreyhound.com

1234 N. Any Street
Chicago, IL 66666
123.456.7890

Lorem ipsum dolor sit amet, consectetur adipiscing elit, sed do eiusmod tempor **incididunt ut** labore et dolore magna aliqua.

Ut enim ad minim veniam, quis nostrud exercitation **ullamco** laboris nisi ut aliquip ex ea commodo consequat. Duis aute irure dolor in reprehenderit in **voluptate velit** esse cillum.

experience

3.2012 - present ◄

Role Four at Company Four

- Lorem ipsum **dolor sit amet**, consectetur adipiscing elit, sed do eiusmod tempor.
- Incididunt ut labore et dolore magna aliqua. Ut enim ad **minim veniam**, quis nostrud exercitation ullamco laboris nisi ut aliquip ex ea commodo consequat.
- Duis aute irure dolor in reprehenderit in **voluptate** velit esse.

8.2010 - 3.2012 ◄

Role Three at Company Three

- Lorem ipsum dolor sit amet, consectetur adipiscing elit, sed do eiusmod tempor.
- Incididunt ut **labore** et dolore magna aliqua. Ut enim ad minim veniam, quis.
- Nostrud exercitation ullamco laboris nisi ut aliquip ex ea **commodo** consequat.

4.2006 - 7.2010 ◄

Role Two at Company Two

- Lorem ipsum dolor sit amet, consectetur adipiscing elit, sed do eiusmod tempor.
- Incididunt ut labore et **dolore** magna aliqua. Ut enim ad minim veniam, quis nostrud exercitation ullamco laboris nisi ut aliquip ex ea commodo consequat.

6.2004 - 3.2006 ◄

Role One at Company One

- Incididunt ut labore et dolore magna aliqua. Ut enim ad **minim veniam**, quis nostrud **exercitation** ullamco laboris nisi ut aliquip ex ea commodo consequat.
- Lorem ipsum dolor sit amet, consectetur adipiscing elit, sed do eiusmod tempor.

education

2000-2004 ◄

University of Awesome
Degree, focus of study

linkedin.com/in/jetgreyhound

skills

Skill one, this is skill two, skill three, this is skill four, skill five, this is skill six, skill seven, this is skill eight, skill nine

FIG 6: THE EXAMPLE RÉSUMÉ DESIGN OF JET GREYHOUND.

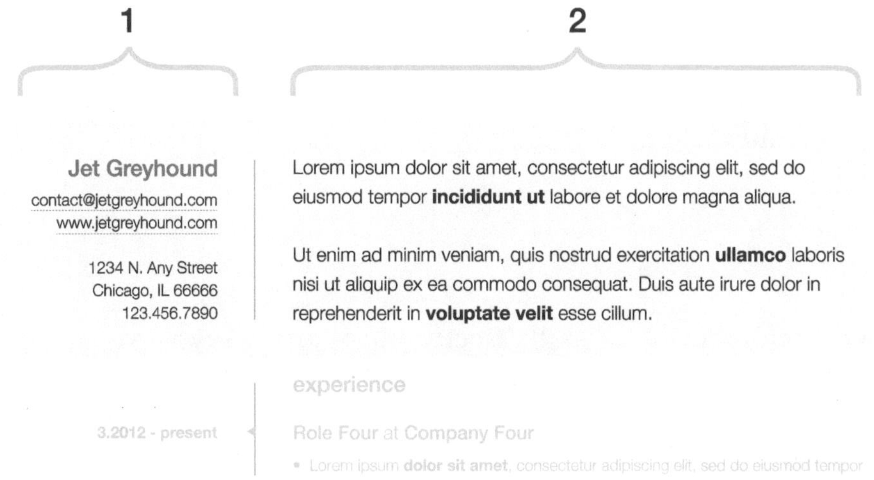

FIG 6.1: THE TOP HIERARCHICAL POSITION OF THE DESIGN IS GIVEN TO JET'S VALUABLE CONTACT INFORMATION AND SUMMARY.

Make the Sought After Into the Readily Apparent

Next let's discuss hierarchy. Immediately within the top 20% of the design is a quick-hit global impression of who Jet is and what he offers (FIG 6.1):

1. Name, portfolio URL, and contact information
2. A few brief sentences that can note things like education, influences, capabilities, or goals

With education already tipped off, we can proceed directly into the next tier of hierarchy an employer is looking for: what is Jet's experience, and how does it relate to the position to which he's applying? Leveraging a timeline design can be an immediate visual cue as to how this information is segmented out. There are other cues we can employ: underlining links, for example. We're already trained to think "I can click this" when we see text underlined on a web site. Amongst the content of your résumé, this helps the viewer find where they can view more information, or contact you, quickly.

Bolding words or phrases you feel a potential employer shouldn't miss—as they relate to your background and experience—is another way to enhance scannability amongst your résumé content.

Finish Strong

Wrapping up with a "skills" section provides a keyword-type benefit, again facilitating a quick-scan global view of capabilities. In reality, "skills" could also be memberships, accomplishments, publications, or any other similar supplementary content that rounds out what you feel is pertinent to the role which you're applying for.

Referencing a "more information" URL immediately to the left of skills in this example qualifies that if the potential employer would like to dig a bit deeper, the means to do so is directly present. In particular with that LinkedIn URL, Jet is able to keep the résumé clean and recent to his most current (and relevant) roles. If the résumé reader wants an exhaustive account of his career, recommendations, and a full skill set listing, they clearly have that ability. From a résumé submission perspective, having a fully completed, detailed LinkedIn profile (that you can provide a link to) is valuable to qualify your "full story". That said, the related link could also reference a page on your portfolio site that contains more information about you, your work, or your process, as well.

These methods of making your résumé more usable to a potential employer are conducive to any type of design; this layout is merely an example. However, by ensuring your résumé is an immediately scannable, hierarchical read, you're making it far easier amongst a deluge of submissions to be noted for your abilities, drive, and experience.

The Mutual Interview

Be it via job application, follow-up phone call, or on-site conversation, an interview always comes before signing on the dotted line. This interview is a mutual dialogue, not an interrogation.

There will be the staple questions: talking through your background, experience, and body of work. "How much notice would you need to give to your current employer (if you're presently employed)?" "Tell me about an area you feel you need improvement?"

(As a side note to the last question: should that one come up, ultimately reflect it back to the business. Transparency would yield a genuine answer in return.)

Those stock questions have their business value. But, you also have to consider what's not being asked. Have you been asked about who inspires you in what you do? What fulfills you and has helped you grow in your work? What you read to stay on top of your craft's evolution? How often you attend (or speak at) events, lectures, or meet-ups? A creative culture cares deeply about these things.

My friends, this conversation is where you must dig deep. Be thoughtfully tenacious. In advance of the interview, pick a few things that are of utmost importance to you and to doing your best work. For example, the ability to work offsite. Or, a description of the team's design process. What about how employees are onboarded? Make sure that those are the things you spend plenty of time asking questions about, and of varied interview participants; different people offer different perspectives.

You: *"Do people work from coffee shops?"*
Business: *"Of course!"*
You: *"That's great to hear. Which ones? How long are they able to work there? Are there any particular days they can't do that? Why?"*

In advance of the interview, pick a few things that are of utmost importance to you and to doing your best work.

If you ask about how you'd be welcomed into the company and culture on your first day, do they have an immediate, detailed, and passionate retort? If the question gets met with stumbles, shrugged shoulders, or flop sweat, that part of their process is likely not thoughtfully cared for.

Keep Your Head on a Swivel

Beyond this dialogue, consider the fact that a "day in the life" of the respective company is effectively unfolding before your eyes at that point, plainly and openly. The spatial observations during an interview are equally paramount to establishing a cultural connection.

If you're not offered a tour of the office, ask to be shown around. What can you spot in the space? We all exercise hyper self-awareness during an interview: *Was that handshake too hard? Am I speaking slowly enough? Do I have salad in my teeth?* Once in the offices of a company you're interested in, however, give equal awareness to your surroundings.

We're talking about basic human observation, a process so vital to the craft of human-centered design. Are people having conversations over coffee? Are they scuttling off to meeting rooms? Collaboratively sketching or whiteboarding? Are they smiling? Are they sullen? Take heed of these snapshots as a collective sampling, and compare that picture against the company's story and what you've ascertained from your interview conversation.

Being ever-cognizant of what's important to you to do your best work, take in what you see of the workspace and office layout, too. Ask questions about what you observe. Are there places for people to work away from their desks? Is management seated in offices or with everyone else? Is there an area for people to creatively reset their energy? As with the interview conversation, probe deeper about what's most important to you.

The Mutual Win

The interview process is for pragmatic investigation. You've made it to the point of having a discussion, and the dialogue you'll be having is exactly that: a conversation, not an interrogation. Use this time to be thoughtful, observant, inquisitive, and above all else, true to yourself and the passion for your craft.

And this is what it's really all about in the end: you. Your work is an extension of yourself. Your **best** work will come from the support and challenge a creative culture will consistently provide you.

Conclusion

It's all about people.

It's paramount that we're compassionate and inclusive as we design, while we develop, and in what we ultimately deliver into the world for people to experience. People on your team, those you pass in the hallway, and co-workers you break bread with at the lunch table deserve those same values. *You* deserve the same. And that's why this is imperative:

Don't settle. Take your Sunday evenings back; they can exist without anxiety. It can be a night of anticipation of the week ahead and revisiting the previous one in your mind with the humble recognition of what you've accomplished.

Don't settle. Instead of looking back on years of compromised work and industry burnout, seek out the companies who are doing it right. They're out there. The passion for doing your best work is too precious to be extinguished by an unhealthy culture. The human beings on the receiving end of the experiences we're crafting can't settle for anything less.

Don't settle for a hushed voice. For ego. For a design process that rushes product to the finish line at the expense of those who ultimately use it. For many companies and individuals, perceptual and procedural shifts abound in this book. For businesses, how employee time is tracked and measured. For employees, harnessing the tangible to inform the intangible.

When **human-centered interactions** are at the center of a creative culture, humility and equality bring us out of the dark ages—where a worker is relegated to an undervalued, dehumanized production machine.

When **human-centered design** drives our creative process, inclusion of those we're crafting for supersedes designing in a vacuum—where success is defined by how close a product interface matches the C-suite's napkin sketch.

Across quality of work and quality of life, the result of always putting people first is nothing short of industry transformation.

About the Author

Justin is a multi-faceted, multi-pierced, multi-tattooed designer, author, and speaker. With Josef Müller-Brockmann and user advocacy claiming equal parts of his creative heart since graduating The School of the Art Institute of Chicago, he's immersed himself in tangible and digital media over the past 20 years.

Justin is fueled by engaging with people on the human-centered connection: speaking at events, at businesses, on podcasts, in articles, etc. The process and strategy of design and culture—individually and in unison—largely inform his passion.

You can reach out to him, or find more information, via the below outlets:

 @pseudoroom
pseudoroom.com

 @the_culturebook
the-culturebook.com

Acknowledgements

Above all else, inarticulable gratitude to my wife Kaity for the room to write, think, and to stare into space blankly when cohesive thoughts proved elusive. Keeping our two children happily amused and engaged for hours on end while I toiled away on this book is a gift I'm ever-grateful for.

Massive appreciation to my friend and colleague Jaan Orvet for the ever-dependable ear, brilliance, and confidence; truly the Yoda of human-centered creative culture (in wisdom and Force knowledge, not stature or age).

Jeffrey Zeldman's council, candor, trust, and respect proved the impetus for this project; from its humble origins as an *A List Apart* article through a self-published work. Katel LeDu and Lisa Maria Martin provided absolutely invaluable structural and tone-of-voice guidance at the onset of writing, tightening my work and broadening my thinking then and onward. Ann Maynard's wit, editorial genius, and stunning insights brought this book from the minor leagues to the big show. Despite plentiful commitments, yet without hesitation, Steve Portigal graciously crafted an introduction to the second edition that beautifully interweaves his invaluable insights with the book's core themes.

The copious conceptual brainstorming sessions with Bobby Price were creative fuel for the soul. His illustrative work and raw talent legitimately brought this book to life. Michael Glascott's illustrations for this second edition were the icing on the cake, helping me bring the comic book panel concept to beautiful fruition.

Andreas Carlsson, my brother in design from Linköping, endlessly opened my mind, challenged me to think bigger, and called me on my bullshit (with much appreciation and necessity). Nansen introduced me to Swedish culture in business—and in lifestyle—both in Chicago and Stockholm; experiences and opportunities that had value beyond measure. Ben Cox, my brother from the South, kindly introduced me to Nick Sarillo.

I'm beyond thankful to Nick for the window into his business, humble genius, and incredible story. Andy Budd provided his industry defining thoughts and insights for this book; his cultural initiatives have been cornerstone inspirations. Sara Cantor Aye and George Aye lent me their time, their brilliance, and the use of their studio space in the midst of a busy morning. They selflessly donated their time and energy to me, and this topic, due to their collective passion for human-centered work environments, design process, and people being treated fairly and respectfully.

In a tactile sense, my iPad Pro proved to be the ultimate tool for wordsmithing, sketching concepts, and toting to my favorite cafés. High five, Apple. And to those emporiums of caffeine and tranquility whose seats I warmed for hours on end, big ups to Soho House, Hero Coffee, Dollop, Star Lounge, and Standing Passengers.

Lastly, thank you to the city of Chicago, my birthplace and home, for serving up unending inspiration through art, music, and culture. Functioning as the backdrop for much of this book's content and interactions, I can't imagine having written it in any other place.

References

Chapter 1

State of Mind at Work by Tommie Cau and Jaan Orvet
http://www.stateofmindatwork.com

Inside Apple by Adam Lashinsky
https://www.amazon.com/Inside-Apple-Americas-Admired-Secretive-Company/
dp/145551215X

Chapter 2

Egonomics by David Marcum and Steven Smith
https://www.amazon.com/egonomics-Makes-Greatest-Expensive-Liability/
dp/1416533273

"The Costs of Ego" by Dr. Maynard Brusman
https://www.scribd.com/document/137063530/The-Costs-of-Ego

*First, Break All the Rules: What the World's Greatest Managers Do
Differently* by Marcus Buckingham
https://www.amazon.com/First-Break-All-Rules-Differently/dp/1595621113/

"Jeong Kwan," *Chef's Table: Volume 3,* Netflix, 2017
https://www.netflix.com/title/80007945

Chapter 3

Drift Volume 4: Stockholm
https://driftmag.com/products/volume-4-stockholm

"Why Lego's CEO Thinks More Grown-Ups Should Play at Work"
by Jo Cofino in *The Huffington Post*

http://www.huffingtonpost.com/entry/lego-and-the-power-of-play-to-transform-business_us_55d72809e4b020c386de52bd

Play by Dr. Stuart Brown
https://www.amazon.com/Play-Shapes-Brain-Imagination-Invigorates/dp/1583333789

Chapter 4

"Employee trust and workplace performance" by Sarah Brown, Daniel Gray, Jolian McHardy, and Karl Taylor in the *Journal of Economic Behavior & Organization*
http://www.sciencedirect.com/science/article/pii/S0167268115001365

"It's ok to say what's ok" by Giles Turnbull on the Government Digital Service blog
https://gds.blog.gov.uk/2016/05/25/its-ok-to-say-whats-ok/

"Old Faithful" by Sheena D'lima in *Better Interiors*
http://www.betterinteriors.in/old-faithful-2/902/

"Working Best at Coffee Shops" by Conor Friedersdorf in *The Atlantic*
http://www.theatlantic.com/business/archive/2011/04/working-best-at-coffee-shops/237372/

Chapter 5

Effective Public Relations by Scott M. Cutlip
https://www.goodreads.com/book/show/477420.Effective_Public_Relations

The Field Guide to Human-Centered Design by IDEO.org
http://www.designkit.org/resources/1

Why Work Sucks and How to Fix It: The Results-Only Revolution by Cali Ressler and Jody Thompson

https://www.amazon.com/Why-Work-Sucks-How-Fix/dp/1591842921

"4 Ways To Create A Human-Centered Workplace, Notes From An Operations Manager" by Samantha Kawabata on the Greater Good Studios blog

https://medium.com/greater-good-studio/4-ways-to-create-a-human-centered-workplace-notes-from-an-operations-manager-dd049e77dc19

HUMAN~CENTERED
INTERACTION, DESIGN, & INSPIRATION

the-culturebook.com

The book's online home features the Creative Culture podcast of conversations with thought leaders and cultural beacons. The site also houses the Creative Culture blog, the latest news, links, and more.

@the_culturebook

www.the-culturebook.com
@the_culturebook

CPSIA information can be obtained
at www.ICGtesting.com
Printed in the USA
LVHW072141080720
660158LV00015B/1849